Green School Primer
LESSONS IN SUSTAINABILITY

images
Publishing

Published in Australia in 2009 by
The Images Publishing Group Pty Ltd
ABN 89 059 734 431
6 Bastow Place, Mulgrave, Victoria 3170, Australia
Tel: +61 3 9561 5544 Fax: +61 3 9561 4860
books@imagespublishing.com
www.imagespublishing.com

National Library of Australia Cataloguing-in-Publication entry:

Title:	Green school primer: lessons in sustainability / compiler, LPA Inc.
ISBN:	9781864703276
Subjects:	Schools – Design and construction.
	Sustainable buildings – Design and construction.
	Architecture and energy conservation – Handbooks, manuals, etc.
	Sustainable architecture.
Other Authors/Contributors:	LPA (Firm)
Dewey Number:	720.47

Coordinating editor: Robyn Beaver

Designed by The Graphic Image Studio Pty Ltd, Mulgrave, Australia
www.tgis.com.au

Pre-publishing services by Splitting Image Colour Studio Pty Ltd, Australia
Printed on FSC-certified paper by Everbest Printing Co. Ltd., in Hong Kong/China

Mixed Sources
Product group from well-managed
forests, and other controlled sources
www.fsc.org Cert no. SGS-COC-003563
© 1996 Forest Stewardship Council
FSC

Contents

Foreword

Marvin J. Malecha, FAIA
Dean, North Carolina State University College of Design
2009 President, The American Institute of Architects

School design has a rich history in our nation. It has attracted the attention of some of our best minds and an ample body of knowledge now exists to demonstrate that there is a clear connection between a well-designed learning environment and the performance of both students and faculty. This should be no surprise to us, because this is a lesson learned over and over again in industry and business. Design makes a difference. When we invest in the careful design of any environment, we are making an investment in our spirit. The investment in our youth can be marked by the investment in the schools that frame a substantial portion of their lives. The importance of school building in the community is a signal as to the importance that education has within a society.

When Thomas Jefferson set out to find a place for his own interest in learning, he devoted the final portion of his life to the foundation and design of the University of Virginia. It is important to note that he took great care to not only frame the legislation for the University in terms of the curriculum to be offered, but also with a detailed physical description of the buildings that would comprise the campus. He realized a physical setting where the buildings themselves became a starting point for learning.

Today, our designs for school buildings offer the same opportunity. However, our challenge is no longer the communication of an architectural language that would give a sense of timelessness to the nation. Our challenge today is to address the urgent environmental crisis looming. Never have we been required to address the questions of environmental well-being, sustainability, and the connected question of human health with such a sense of urgency. How we build will have a substantial effect on the success of our efforts to meet this challenge. We must learn to live differently from the dependency that has arisen among us for built environments operating with little or no synchronization with the natural environment.

This is what makes the joining of the school building type and the strategies to live in harmony with the land so compelling. There is a possibility that the lessons learned in school—making the manipulation of a building obvious to students, faculty, and visitors alike—will actually embed a way of living in the community for the benefit of all and for the restoration of the environment.

While this book is the result of the work of a single architecture firm, it is a case for the power of architects to address the most important issues of our time. It is for this reason that I recommend this book to public officials, school officials, and colleague architects.

The development of a primer is a fitting model for the endeavor of creating this monograph. It is an introduction to principles even as it uses sophisticated finished products as exemplars. The goal is as much an articulation of ideas as it is finished products, and it allows for the reader, no matter how experienced, to make leaps of understanding.

The approach is straightforward. First, the concept of green is explored by definition and by benefits to specific constituencies, including the regulatory influences context for building. Importantly, the second section addresses building and operating costs. This is followed by an assessment of green rating systems and their applicability to the design of schools. With this groundwork accomplished, sustainable principles are articulated, in the tradition of a primer, in language that can be embraced by architects and school officials alike. The substance of the text follows as case studies are offered to demonstrate the applications of these principles. The exemplars include new construction as well as renovation projects. All of the projects are presented in the context of green priorities.

I have been familiar with the work of LPA, Inc. for more than 25 years. It does not surprise me that it has continued to grow and mature as an architectural leader in the area of green design. My earliest memory of this firm is of a community willing to explore and experiment in practice and in design collaborations. The venturesome and collaborative spirit that has been evident in this office has continued to find its voice in the green imperative now before our nation and the world. This is a group of individuals who have committed themselves to design thinking with a mind to address the most pressing problem of our age. It is fitting that this volume is dedicated to school design; there is much for us to learn among its pages.

CHAPTER 1

A Green School Primer

The U.S. is enjoying a school construction boom.

In 2000, U.S. school districts spent approximately $21.6 billion on new school construction and upgrades and/or enlargements of existing schools, according to the 33rd Annual Official Education Construction Report. In 2006, school districts spent $25.3 billion. School districts are projected to spend $51.4 billion on new construction, modernization, and expansion projects between 2007 and 2009.

As of June 25, 2008, California's Office of Public School Construction had approved more than $12 billion in K–12 new construction and modernization projects for the state.

In the midst of this boom, school districts have a remarkable opportunity not only to build new facilities and enhance existing classrooms, but to accommodate 21st-century teaching and learning modalities and to improve the programming of school functions, adjacencies, and amenities.

They can also improve the health of their students, teachers, and administrators, save money, and make one of our planet's most important issues—the environment—a daily, compelling part of our children's lives and educational experience.

How? By constructing new "green" schools and performing green modernizations on existing educational buildings.

What makes a school green?

Green schools are healthier places to learn and work, they have minimal negative impact on the environment, and they have lower overhead costs compared to conventional schools.

To be green, a school interior must have abundant natural daylighting, outdoor views, high indoor air quality, good acoustics, and a comfortable temperature.

A green school is constructed with sustainable building materials, such as steel with significant recycled content, rapidly renewable materials like bamboo and cork, and products from paints to glues that do not "off-gas" the toxic volatile organic compounds (VOCs) often found in conventional building materials. Natural linoleum made from linseed oil and jute—rather than conventional dioxin-laden vinyl composition tile—for example, is non-toxic, attractive, durable, and also highly recyclable at the end of its useful life.

Instead of particleboard, which is made with toxic formaldehyde-based resins that have been linked to a wide variety of respiratory and other illnesses, cabinets and shelves in each classroom can be made with a wide variety of more sustainable products, including low-VOC medium density fiberboard (MDF), Forest Stewardship Council (FSC)-certified wood, and strawboard, a highly renewable agricultural byproduct.

A green school has energy-efficient buildings systems, particularly its lighting and HVAC (heating, ventilation, air conditioning) systems. Often, a green school uses natural ventilation strategies that provide fresh air without use of the primary HVAC system, which reduces energy consumption and costs.

A green school significantly reduces water consumption compared to a conventional school using strategies like water-conserving plumbing fixtures, drought-tolerant landscaping, and water-conserving irrigation systems like drip irrigation and low precipitation rate spray heads and bubblers.

The planning and design of a green school furthers its energy efficiency and water conservation, reduces use of natural resources, and lowers its negative environmental impact.

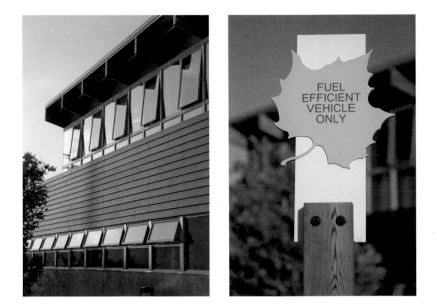

Green site planning, for example, minimizes grading, which reduces the likelihood of erosion. A green school's building orientation makes the most of sunlight (natural daylighting, warmth in winter) and wind (natural ventilation). Landscaping shades exterior walls, reducing the need for air conditioning in the summer and heating in the winter.

A green school is also a genuine living laboratory where students and educators expand their environmental understanding and conservation activities far beyond contributing to classroom recycling bins. The schools themselves are educational tools.

Contrary to popular opinion, schools don't have to be new to be green. Existing conventional schools—there are more than 126,000 of them in the U.S.—can undergo a green modernization, spreading healthier and more efficient educational facilities to every corner of our communities.

The benefits of going green

Green schools are the ultimate example of a win–win situation. They benefit everyone from students to teachers, administrators, school districts, their communities, and the planet.

Benefits for students

"When you consider the fact that 50 million young people spend eight hours a school day in a school building, we should do everything we can

to make that environment work for them, not against them," says Michelle Moore, a Senior Vice President of the U.S. Green Building Council (USGBC). "Parents, teachers, and school board officials understand better than anyone the link between child health and learning; and the fact is that children in green schools have fewer sick days and better test scores."

Conventional schools—old and new—suffer from often minimal daylighting and outdoor views, and particularly from the toxic off-gassing of traditional building materials (often exacerbated by poor ventilation systems) that has been linked to health problems from headaches and colds to asthma and weakened immune systems.

Green schools, however, provide a much healthier indoor environment, which means fewer illnesses and lower illness-related absenteeism rates.

Students also perform better in green schools. Studies by the Heschong Mahone Group, Inc. documented a 10 to 21 percent improvement in learning rates and test scores in students who had classrooms with natural light, superior indoor air quality, and outdoor views, when compared to students in classrooms with minimal natural daylight.

At many green schools, students also have hands-on learning environments where they can study ecosystems, alternative power generation, or even organic gardening. At the Hector Godinez Fundamental High School in Santa Ana, California, for example, the campus has a nature center—an open space preserve with a small wetlands—that serves, among other uses, as an educational tool for the adjacent science classrooms.

Benefits for teachers

A healthier indoor environment means that teachers and administrators also have fewer illnesses and lower absenteeism rates in green schools compared to conventional schools.

Abundant natural daylighting and outdoor views help teachers to be more productive, to perform better, and to have higher job satisfaction rates.

Benefits for administrators, school boards, and school districts

One-third of a school's costs are in heating and cooling, water consumption, electricity, and other power sources. A green building reduces energy consumption by up to 40 percent, and sometimes more, and it lowers water consumption by up to 50 percent or more compared to a conventional building. The U.S. Green Building Council claims that a green school saves on average $100,000 per year compared to a conventional school.

The Ohio School Facilities Commission adopted the LEED for Schools rating system (see Chapter 3) into its school design standards. The Commission estimates that it will save $1.4 billion over the next 40 years just by reducing the energy consumption of the state's schools.

Because green schools reduce overhead costs, administrators and school districts have more money to allocate for the purchase of new textbooks or computers or even for the hiring of more teachers.

Green schools could spell the end of fundraising bake sales.

And the benefits for school boards and school districts don't end there.

Green schools generate higher student test scores, which help school districts meet state and federal standards.

Green schools also have lower teacher absenteeism and turnover rates. One green school in Montgomery County, Maryland, the Great Seneca Creek Elementary School, had a zero percent teacher turnover rate in the 2007–2008 school year.

Finally, green schools help school boards and school districts meet the growing demand for tangible public actions to reduce our nation's dependency on foreign oil, to lower greenhouse gas emissions, and combat global climate change.

Benefits for the environment

On average, green schools use 33 percent less energy, consume 32 percent less water, reduce solid waste by 74 percent, and have lower greenhouse gas emissions than comparable conventional schools.

That's 33 percent less use of fossil fuel power sources, which lowers greenhouse gas emissions and helps to combat global climate change.

Water is becoming an increasingly precious natural resource, particularly in regions like southern California that are struggling with long-term drought. The more water our schools don't use, the better for the environment—and our long-term potable water supplies.

Using salvaged building materials, materials with significant recycled content, and rapidly renewable materials means fewer natural resources are consumed for the construction of a new school, or for the green modernization of an existing conventional school, which preserves those natural resources for the other species on this planet, and for future generations.

Green building materials are as durable—and in some cases, more durable—than conventional building products, which means they don't have to be replaced every year or two, further conserving natural resources.

Green building rating systems are also beginning to adopt criteria mandating the recyclability of a building at the end of its useful life. The 2009 update to CHPS (see Chapter 3), for example, includes "design for deconstruction," that is, planning and designing a building so that it can be easily renovated and adapted to future needs, and then deconstructed and recycled at the end of its useful life, which will also conserve natural resources.

Green school drivers

All of the benefits discussed above are major drivers of the shift to green schools. And there are more.

Local, regional, state, federal, and utility company grants, rebates, and other incentives are also driving green schools. In northern California, the Pacific Gas & Electric (PG&E) utility company provides rebates for the installation of many energy-efficient components, up to the full cost of the equipment purchase price.

Savings By Design—a program sponsored for several years by four of California's largest utilities under the auspices of the Public Utilities Commission—has encouraged high-performance non-residential building design and construction by providing a range of services, including design assistance, incentives to help offset the costs of energy-efficient building features, and design team incentives that reward designers who meet ambitious energy efficiency targets.

California's $100 million Proposition 1D High Performance Incentive Program provides funding for new K–12 school construction, modernizations, and relocations that incorporate the efficient use of water, energy, and natural resources and that provide superior indoor air quality, acoustics, and lighting.

A growing number of government regulations are also driving the shift to green schools. Dozens of cities and counties in California have mandated green building criteria for new construction and major renovation public projects, including Alameda (city and county), Anaheim, Berkeley, Burbank, Calabasas, Costa Mesa, Irvine, Long Beach, Los Angeles (city and county), Oakland, Pasadena, Sacramento, San Bernardino County, San Francisco, San Jose, and Santa Monica.

California's AB 32, the 2006 Global Warming Solutions Act, mandates cutting the state's carbon dioxide emissions to its 1990 level—or a 30 percent reduction—by 2020. As buildings generate 48 percent of U.S. carbon dioxide emissions, the state has begun drafting new regulations that target building greenhouse gas emissions, which will directly impact schools.

The U.S. House of Representatives has established the new Green Schools Caucus co-chaired by Rep. Darlene Hooley (D-OR), Rep. Michael McCaul (R-TX), and Rep. Jim Matheson (D-UT). The Caucus was created to raise awareness about the benefits of green schools within Congress, to drive policy discussions, and to generate legislative opportunities.

Green is the color of the future. We've got the money, we've got the knowledge, we've got the construction materials and mechanical systems, and we've got the experience to create new green schools and carry out green modernizations of conventional schools. Our children, educators, school districts, communities, and the planet all win.

What are we waiting for?

CHAPTER 2

The Truth About Green School Costs

Green is really about defining the value system a school will embody. Green has little to do with changes in a project's budget. It is about how that budget is used to effect change.

Many people believe the pervasive myth that green schools cost much more than conventional schools, and that green is a high-priced luxury school districts cannot afford.

The truth, however, is that the cost of well-designed green schools is comparable to that of their conventional counterparts.

A 2006 study of 30 new green schools by the U.S. Green Building Council (USGBC) found that those educational facilities cost on average just 1.65 percent more than comparable conventional schools.

The 2007 Davis Langdon *Cost of Green Revisited* study found that "there is no significant difference in average costs for green buildings as compared to non-green buildings … Average construction costs have risen dramatically the past three years—between 25% and 30%. And yet we still see a large number of projects achieving LEED [green building certification] within budget." (See Chapter 3 for more about LEED.)

Since 2003, the GSA, the Federal Government's landlord, has been constructing new green buildings on the conventional construction budgets authorized by Congress.

The Collaborative for High Performance Schools (CHPS) (see Chapter 3) estimates that its standards add as little as $1.50 per square foot to construction budgets, including soft costs. The overall added costs for a CHPS school are estimated to run from 0 to 2.5 percent of the budget, excluding the cost of the land. The long-term paybacks, however, are estimated at *10 to 20* times the initial construction costs in lower energy and water costs, reduced maintenance costs, and greater teacher attraction and retention, among many other benefits.

Falling green school costs

Certainly, green buildings cost more than conventional buildings when they first began appearing in the U.S. in the late 1990s. Sustainable building materials were few and far between, high-efficiency building systems and other green technologies were new and expensive. Of equal importance, architects, engineers, contractors, and real estate industry professionals were learning about green buildings on the job, which raised both the construction time and cost of a green project.

That was then, this is now.

The marketplace has exploded with a wide variety of green building materials, building systems, and technologies, which has made them very cost competitive with conventional building products. Recycled carpets and ceiling tiles, for example, were once priced at a premium, but no longer.

Indirect lighting fixtures with daylight controls provide a higher light level using less energy and generate less heat than conventional fixtures, thereby reducing air conditioning costs and the need to replace lamps as frequently. Indirect lighting fixtures were priced at a premium eight years ago. Today, the cost is comparable to long-standard, but hotter and less efficient, parabolic lighting.

Building materials with significant recycled content, like carpeting, are now competitively priced with conventional building materials.

Middle and bottom: Raised floor air distribution system, under construction and completed.

A raised floor air distribution system, which delivers air to a room at a lower level, allowing natural stratification to occur, was twice as expensive eight years ago as it is today. This system also uses significantly less energy than the traditional system of forcing air down from the ceiling plenum, which saves money.

Of critical importance, thousands of architects, engineers, contractors, and other real estate industry professionals are now both knowledgeable about and experienced in new green construction and green modernizations of conventional buildings. The learning curve—and cost—have gone.

Green school incentives

Helping to lower the cost of new green schools and the green modernizations of conventional schools are a growing number of government jurisdictions and utility companies providing help, design advice, and a wide variety of incentives to turn schools and other buildings green.

Savings By Design, for example, is a California-wide utility-sponsored program that has provided incentives for energy (gas and electricity) conservation beyond the state's Title 24 Energy Efficiency Code criteria. Its successor, the Sustainable Communities Program, is being offered by all California utility companies between 2009 and 2013. This new program provides incentives over and above those found in Savings By Design for those projects pursuing LEED and/or CHPS ratings (see Chapter 3).

Other incentives are available throughout California. The Los Angeles Department of Water and Power provides a Green Building Incentive of up to $250,000 to help make buildings greener. The Sacramento Municipal Utility District provides incentives for the installation of energy-efficient air conditioning and lighting systems and a design stipend for projects using an integrated design approach (see Chapter 4).

The California Energy Commission's Bright Schools Program offers loans with a 3 percent interest rate to help finance green modernization projects.

Through the Proposition 1D High Performance Incentive Program, California's Department of General Services' Office of Public School Construction provides $100 million in High Performance Incentive Grants for green schools.

The Student Recreation Center at Sonoma State University in Rohnert Park, California was designed using LEED-Silver criteria. Natural daylighting, natural ventilation with a night flushing system, insulated Low-E windows, wood trellis canopies, and built-in seating with night flushing vents are among the many strategies that helped to make the facility 40 percent more energy efficient than required by California's Title 24 energy code.

The Truth About Green School Costs

Long-term operating costs

When it comes to understanding the true costs of green schools, it is important to look at a school's entire lifecycle, not just the upfront construction costs.

A green school has lower operating costs over the short *and* long term compared to a conventional school, which must be incorporated into a school's budgets for facilities management, educational programs, and capital improvements if a school district is going to understand and value the true lifecycle costs that impact it now and in the future.

According to the U.S. Department of Energy's Rebuild America K–12 Schools Program, for example, school energy costs are approximately $100 per student annually. If you add in the costs of water, wastewater processing, and trash, that cost is raised to $125 per student. Green schools can reduce those costs by up to $50 per student. Annually.

Because power, water, maintenance, and other facility costs are lower in green schools, those schools have more money available for what's really needed: teachers' salaries and supplies, textbooks, classroom computers, and other needs directly related to student success.

The average CHPS school, for example, saves 30 percent annually on utilities, which is equivalent to the salaries of two teachers each year.

Certainly, some green building materials, design, and technology choices can cost more initially than conventional choices. Low emission (Low-E) window glazing, for example, costs more than standard glazing. But Low-E glazing helps to reduce HVAC energy consumption and costs by minimizing interior solar heat gain, which will pay for the extra cost of that glazing in a few years, and then continue to reduce energy costs in the years to come.

Other cost issues

Because green schools are healthier than conventional schools, students have fewer illnesses, creating more revenue for the school by increasing the average daily attendance rates. A North Carolina study, for example, found that students in classrooms with abundant natural daylight attended school 3.2 to 3.8 days more per year than students in conventional schools.

In addition, healthier green schools can also avoid the growing litigation plaguing school districts. In California, for example, a student claimed that he had been harmed by "contaminated air" in his junior high school classroom. He filed a lawsuit and received a cash settlement. One-third of the staff in that same conventional school filed workers' compensation claims for respiratory and other health problems.

Low-E window glazing coupled with a sunshade system significantly reduces interior solar heat gain.

CHAPTER 3

Green School Rating Programs

Helping school boards and school districts construct truly green schools and carry out sustainable modernizations of conventional schools are two leading rating programs: LEED for Schools and CHPS.

The LEEDing green building assessment method

The U.S. Green Building Council (www.usgbc.org) was founded in 1993. This respected and independent agency—a coalition of organizations from the real estate industry, government, nonprofit organizations, and schools—began with approximately 300 members and a determination to represent and advocate green buildings and to create a third-party certification program for green buildings. Now, with more than 15,000 member organizations, the USGBC is literally changing the built environment in the U.S. and around the world with its LEED (Leadership in Energy and Environmental Design) program and rating system, which it launched in 2000.

LEED is a demanding program with stringent criteria that guides the planning and construction of a green building, and then evaluates a facility's performance over its life cycle, in six categories: Sustainable Site, Water Efficiency, Energy and Atmosphere, Materials and Resources, Indoor Environmental Quality, and Innovation and Design process. The LEED rating system has four award levels: Certification (26–32 points), Silver (33–38 points), Gold (39–51 points), and Platinum (52+ points).

LEED programs now run the gamut of real estate development, from LEED-NC (new construction and major renovations) to LEED-EB O&M (existing buildings operations and maintenance), LEED-CI (commercial interiors), and LEED-ND (neighborhood development).

A balanced approach to building systems assures optimum energy efficiency and a high-quality indoor environment.

In just eight years, LEED has become the standard for green buildings across the U.S. As of September 1, 2008, LEED criteria for public and even private buildings have been adopted by 44 states, 130 cities, 29 counties, and 15 public school jurisdictions. In California, cities as disparate as Los Angeles, Irvine, Pasadena, Sacramento, San Francisco, and Santa Monica have mandated LEED criteria for their public buildings, including schools.

Originally, K–12 schools earned their LEED ratings under the LEED-NC program. Since 2007, however, they have used the LEED for Schools program.

The Livermore High School Agriculture Science and Technology Complex uses a variety of natural ventilation strategies.

While the LEED for Schools program is based on LEED-NC, it was designed to serve the unique nature of the design, construction, and renovation of K–12 schools. Thus, in addition to focusing on issues such as sustainable site selection, brownfield redevelopment, stormwater management, water efficiency, energy conservation, abundant natural daylighting, and a healthy indoor air quality, it also targets things like classroom acoustics, mold prevention, and using the school as a teaching tool.

LEED for School's greatest benefit is its assurance to students, teachers, administrators, school boards, school districts, and their communities that a school is truly, verifiably green, and that it will perform and provide all of the benefits a sustainable school promises.

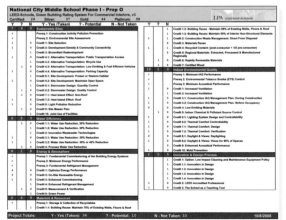

Example of LPA's LID® software program for LEED® for Schools criteria.

Despite its success and growing influence, LEED has had its share of criticism. Many school districts, for example, consider the certification application process too complex and expensive. The Cesar Chavez Elementary School (see Chapter 5), for example, was planned and constructed according to LEED criteria, but the Long Beach Unified School District chose not to apply for LEED certification, deeming the process too costly. It chose, instead, to register Cesar Chavez Elementary School under the CHPS program (see below).

In some cases, the LEED criteria are too narrow in scope. Projects in major cities like New York and San Francisco, for example, lose many opportunities to gain site-related points, because LEED doesn't take into account that it has always been more difficult to construct buildings in major urban centers compared to suburban areas.

In addition, points awarded under the LEED standard often do not reflect the time, cost, and effort given to a green component, which inadvertently encourages architects and developers to pursue LEED points, rather than a greener building. LEED, for example, gives one point for "green power" (renewable energy) and one point for installing walk-off mats at building entrances. Clearly, one strategy is more important than the other when it comes to creating a truly sustainable building, but the LEED program does not yet assign the appropriate weight to key planning, design, and construction measures.

Cesar Chavez Elementary School in Long Beach, California is a CHPS school and the recipient of numerous design awards.

As of September 2008, more than 1,000 public and private schools across the U.S. had been registered for or had received LEED for Schools certification. Currently, one to two schools a day are registering for a LEED for Schools rating.

The Livermore High School Agriculture Science and Technology Complex was designed to meet LEED® for Schools criteria.

The concrete structural frame for El Camino College's new Humanities building reduced the overall building height, required fewer building materials, and conserved natural resources.

Nor does LEED award points to some current green building strategies. The recently completed Humanities building at El Camino College in Torrance, California, for example, was constructed with a concrete structure frame, which reduced the building's overall building height by 5 feet. That height reduction meant that the project needed less construction materials. Thus, fewer natural resources were consumed in building this facility. But LEED does not give points for concrete structure frames and their impact on a building's overall sustainability.

The USGBC, however, has been acting steadily to improve LEED. The newest version, known as LEED 2009, completely changes the credit system, giving greater weight and points to a strategy's potential to either mitigate the negative or promote the positive impacts of a building on the environment and on human beings. LEED 2009 includes a Lifecycle Cost Analysis (LCA), geographic-specific criteria, and it gives more points for energy efficiency and water conservation measures.

The Arcadia (California) High School Performing Arts Center was designed to CHPS standards.

A CHPS scorecard.

CHPS' impact on green schools

The mission of the Collaborative for High Performance Schools (CHPS) is to facilitate the design, construction, and operation of high performance schools: environments that are not only energy and resource efficient, but also healthy, comfortable, well lit, and provide the amenities for a quality education.

Developed before there was a LEED for Schools program, and incorporating many of the LEED criteria into a comprehensive system of environmentally responsible benchmarks, CHPS began in California as America's first green building rating program specifically designed for K–12 schools. CHPS has now spread to seven other states and it has been adopted by several Community College districts.

Currently, more than 30 California school districts require that their new construction and major renovation projects meet CHPS' standards and earn CHPS certification, including Burbank, Long Beach, Los Angeles, Oakland, San Diego, San Francisco, and Visalia.

CHPS has several benefits for school districts. First, California's $100 million Proposition 1D High Performance Incentive Program—which provides funding for new K–12 school construction, modernizations, and relocations—was *based* on CHPS requirements, making it easier for CHPS schools to qualify for the incentives.

Second, because it is a California-based standard, CHPS' criteria align with current state regulations, from the Title 24 Energy Efficiency Standard to SWPPP (Storm Water Pollution Prevention Plan).

Third, unlike LEED for Schools, CHPS has a separate scorecard for modernizations and additions. (LEED will launch a separate green school modernization program in 2009.)

Fourth, like LEED, CHPS is also being updated to reflect the latest advances in green buildings and school district needs. Created in collaboration with the California Energy Commission and U.S. Department of Energy, the 2009 edition of CHPS Criteria for Performance and Operations of Existing Schools will have an assessment tool to allow schools to benchmark their performance in energy, water, acoustics, indoor air quality, and waste usage. They'll also be able to track their operational performance on issues like green cleaning products and methods, transportation, purchasing, and maintenance.

CHPS is also developing a web-based Green Products Database that compares products based on several criteria, including recycled content and VOC levels. In the future, the database will also track Life Cycle Impact Reports, Environmental Product Declarations, and other criteria to encourage and support awareness and understanding of each product's lifecycle.

Like LEED, CHPS also has its challenges. Prior to the 2009 edition, CHPS did not give credit for innovation. Often, this program does not provide the guidelines necessary to help school districts meet specific performance standards. In addition, the client valuing standard for determining commissioning cost is not well defined. The client valuing standard also increases the complexity of a project in documenting credits through an integrated design process early in the project schedule.

In addition, school districts seeking CHPS ratings for major green modernization and expansion projects find that CHPS in the real world is something of an "all or nothing" program and not every school project with multiple programs and functions can take that approach.

Other rating programs

Although LEED is quite dominant in the U.S., and CHPS is growing in importance, they are not the only American green building standards.

The Green Globes program, for example, was imported from Canada by the Green Building Initiative, a Portland, Oregon-based nonprofit organization not to be confused with the United Nations Environment Programme's Green Building Initiative.

Unlike LEED and CHPS, which are independent organizations, the American GBI and the American Green Globes are sponsored by building industry companies. Green Globes began with residential standards, was modified to adopt the National Association of Home Builders' (NAHB's) Model Green Home Building Guidelines, then spread out to the commercial sector. Green Globes does not have a green schools component, it has lax standards and limited credibility, but it is spreading as the GBI tries to make Green Globes a national standard.

More familiar to many people is the EPA's Energy Star program, which focuses on energy efficiency. Energy Star provides tools, such as the Target Finder, that evaluate a project's energy design goals. To earn an Energy Star rating, this program's Portfolio Manager evaluates a project's actual energy efficiency.

Energy Star, however, does not address the full spectrum of green building issues like indoor air quality and non-toxic building materials.

But Energy Star has proven to be an effective program within its purview. The LEED and CHPS programs, for example, have incorporated a variety of Energy Star standards into their criteria.

As more and more stringent energy efficiency and greenhouse gas emissions regulations are enacted, expect LEED and CHPS to place a greater emphasis on Energy Star benchmarking. As former President Bill Clinton states in the Carbon Disclosure Project: "It all begins with keeping score."

The Arcadia (California) High School Performing Arts Center received incentives from the Savings By Design program.

CHAPTER 4

Green School Design Principles and Strategies

LPA, Inc. has made sustainability a part of everything that we do, not only in our work, but also within our company culture. With more than two decades of planning and designing green buildings, LPA, Inc. has developed *10 Sustainable Principles* to guide our work and to inform our clients about the green planning, design, and construction process.

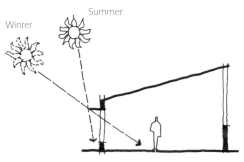

1. Inter+Act

Communication. Collaboration. Cooperation. These three tenets are the essential components of the green planning and design process. Effective and continuous interaction between the architects, landscape architects, engineers, contractors, and the ultimate users and maintenance personnel will ensure a successful design solution.

Any school or school building can be green, functional, beautiful, and completed for no more than the cost of a conventional educational facility. But not if the project team uses the traditional planning and design process, in which the professionals from each discipline—architecture, landscape architecture, engineering, plumbing, lighting, etc.—make stand-alone decisions about their specific aspect of the project independent of the other disciplines.

A school, even a single building, cannot be truly sustainable if it is planned, designed, and constructed using that traditional process.

Why? Unlike traditional territorial thinking, a green building project requires that all of the school's "stakeholders"—from school district staff to school administrators, architects, engineers, faculty, outside consultants,

Roof form provides water collection for rain gauge water feature in courtyard.

> *"Nothing is so simple that it cannot be misunderstood."*
> Freeman Teague, Jr.

maintenance staff, and contractors—be involved in the planning and design process from the very beginning. This promotes a shared understanding of the different school issues and needs that must be addressed in the master plan, as well as green building education and buy-in among all of the stakeholders. These project team members must work together, collaborating and communicating from the very start to create a cost-effective and functional green school.

LPA, Inc. calls this "Sustainable Integrated Design."

Only through communication, collaboration, and cooperation can the disparate needs and concerns of each member of the project team—from programming to curriculum, wayfinding, student social interactions, engineering, lighting, construction, and maintenance—be turned into a single cohesive design that works for everyone over the long term.

By bringing maintenance and operating staff into the planning and design process from the very beginning, for example, they become educated about, and supporters of, every aspect of the green school or building. They will understand and take pride in their role in maintaining, even improving, that sustainability. They'll understand the importance of unplugging a piece of equipment every night to save energy. They'll welcome, appreciate, and use Green Seal cleaning products that are safer and healthier for them to work with, unlike the conventional chemicals that require thick rubber gloves to use and that off-gas toxins that cause respiratory illnesses.

Communication, collaboration, and cooperation are also the core elements of a green school's master plan. Green is not a separate element, and it certainly isn't a gimmick that can be overlaid on a project at the end of the development process, like an architectural cosmetic feature. Each component of a green school Inter+Acts with and supports all of the other components.

Spaces to foster collaboration and embrace daylight.

Green seal cleaning products.

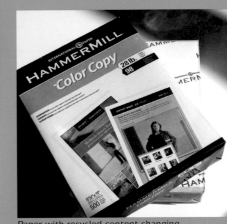

Paper with recycled content changing everyday operations.

21

West-facing louvers reduce heat gain, while still allowing daylight.

Sunscreens on south elevation protect glass and reduce heat gain in student collaboration area.

A green project team understands that sustainability must be integrated into each aspect of the project at the beginning of the planning and design process to make green part of a school's DNA.

Thus, the green planning and design process looks at the entire project and budget as a whole, not as a series of stand-alone elements. Site planning, architectural design, landscape architecture design, and sustainability are one and the same. Similarly, in an *integrated* green planning and design process, there is no artificial distinction between the inside and outside of a building. They are all part of the same system and must work together as collaborative parts of a single whole.

This holistic view of the campus or an individual building shows the project team how the many elements are connected and can work together to create the best green school within the project budget. Thus, the team can manage *up front* the critical interplay of each green component with the rest of the school.

With a green planning and design process, the team can also alter up-front planning and design elements and shift budget allocations from one building component to another to meet budget requirements. The team could, for example, choose to forego a costly and environmentally insignificant feature—such as tackable wall coverings in classrooms—to set aside more of the budget for important green strategies like a displacement ventilation system, which significantly reduces the HVAC system's energy consumption and costs.

Communication, collaboration, and cooperation in the green planning and design process also promote brainstorming and new solutions. You never know where a good idea will come from.

2. Do Less

Minimize your environmental footprint. Conserve natural resources, reduce energy and water consumption, generate less pollution and greenhouse gas emissions, design and build simply with less.

How do you Do Less? Start with conservation. Conserve and protect open space. Reduce the amount of building materials you use, which will conserve natural resources. Choose energy-efficient building systems. Re-think the entire planning and design process so that you provide more sustainability by doing less.

Do Less (*and* save money) by reducing site disturbance and minimizing earthwork (and its negative impact on the environment) by building into or around the landscape, rather than leveling it.

Do Less by minimizing the development footprint. Don't have your school sprawl across a site. That wastes your money and natural resources, and it harms the environment. The less land used by buildings, roads, and parking, the stronger the existing eco-system remains, the less infrastructure is required—reducing the project's initial cost—and the more land is available to absorb stormwater, recharge underground aquifers, prevent heat islands … and provide athletic and recreational amenities.

Build up and down, not out. One two-story building uses less land than two one-story buildings.

Identify joint-use opportunities between the school district and other public and private agencies, such as shared parking, which conserves land.

Do Less by finding the things that are free—LPA, Inc. calls them the "gifts of the site"—and then incorporate those gifts throughout the school design. The sun can provide solar energy and interior daylighting. The wind can support natural ventilation. The school site's topography can help to separate school and community uses, or showcase a particular building function, or promote stormwater management. Existing shade trees can help with heat island mitigation, stormwater management, and school beautification and identity.

Bioswales cleanse stormwater naturally, eliminating the routine maintenance of mechanical treatment systems.

Porous paving allows water to percolate into the groundwater.

Skylight brings daylight into the building core.

One key means of taking advantage of the site's free gifts is building orientation. Of particular importance, building orientation can be used to provide the greatest amount of natural daylighting to the building interior, which will reduce the amount of artificial lighting needed in the facility, and that will lower the project's upfront costs and long-term operating costs.

Similarly, building orientation can maximize the use of prevailing breezes to support natural ventilation, which lowers HVAC system requirements, and therefore both initial and long-term costs.

Each school site is unique, so there's no one-size-fits-all strategy, no single rule or maxim. But by taking advantage of all the "free" gifts of that property through green planning, you will create a school facility that complements not just the entire site, but the surrounding environment as well.

Finally, many schools have smaller budgets and fewer maintenance and building operations staff who are spread much thinner than in the past. So, Do Less by designing and constructing a green school that requires less maintenance and oversight. It doesn't pay to have the educational equivalent of a Ferrari that the mechanic has to tweak all the time to keep it running perfectly.

3. Challenge Convention

Never assume. Never settle. Never accept the status quo. Keep an open mind and explore.

Each green school project should be challenged to provide the most sustainable solution—whether it is simple, new, traditional, or different from the way things have always been done.

Creativity and innovation are vital in the green planning, design, and construction process. Don't be afraid to turn from the tried and true that doesn't work in your particular situation to find a creative sustainable solution for a particular problem or challenge.

When it comes to sustainability, there are no rules of thumb. This doesn't mean, however, that you're going to end up with the most radical solution every time. You simply have the freedom to Challenge Convention. If the traditional method is the right solution, then you choose the traditional method.

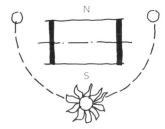

External stairs don't have to be mechanically conditioned, and provide for wayfinding opportunities on a campus.

Joint-use gymnasium embraces natural light.

Challenging Convention requires new ethical standards for the 21st century. This is a very exciting time to work in the building industry, because it brings many new challenges and opportunities. With those opportunities comes great responsibility to refuse to settle for the energy efficiency standards of the past or the unsustainable land and material choices of the 20th century. We must change the world one green project at a time.

The Challenge Convention principle is particularly critical when thinking about and planning how classrooms are used, because classroom use is very different from what it was 50 or 60 years ago. Today, educators are teaching differently and students are learning differently. A classroom needs to support small collaborative groupings. A teacher standing in front of students may no longer be standing at the front of the classroom. Classroom proportions are changing to accommodate new teaching and learning modalities, and also the new technologies, like student computers.

And none of us knows what the teaching and learning process and needs will be five or ten years from now.

So, a green classroom design means a flexible classroom design that can be easily adapted to today's teaching and learning needs, and tomorrow's.

One of the most important conventions the project team should challenge is cookie-cutter architecture for schools. **Design does matter**. It gives the school an identity, connection to the larger community, and creates "pride of ownership" in students, faculty, administrators, and staff. Design enriches their daily lives. Design adds beauty to the community. It matters.

Alternative mechanical systems to the "package unit" can be more efficient, and cost effective.

Exposing structure allows for unique learning opportunities.

Horizontal canopy defines the building entry, and provides shade for outdoor courtyard.

4. Zoom Out

Each school is part of a much larger whole—the surrounding neighborhood, the entire community and its businesses, local higher education institutions, and the environment. The project team must integrate each school's planning, design, construction, and uses into that larger whole.

When you Zoom Out, you start by incorporating the school district's (or city's, or state's) sustainability standards into the green school's master plan.

Zoom Out at the beginning of a project by looking beyond the school site. Conduct a macro examination of adjacent buildings, pedestrian access, roads, the surrounding neighborhood, the larger community, and the environment to understand their impact on the school, and the projected impact of the school on them.

When you Zoom Out, for example, ask yourself: what is the perception of safety in the school's surrounding neighborhood? In most cases, no matter how low the crime rate, residents with school-age children won't think their neighborhood is safe enough. Sadly, in these days of "Amber Alerts," well-designed drop off zones at K–12 schools are a necessity.

When you Zoom Out, you engage the community in the green school planning and design process *and* you take advantage of the opportunities to integrate the school into the community, such as connecting the school to local pedestrian and bicycle trails.

As you Zoom Out, examine how this green school can help solve larger problems within the community, from the lack of sufficient open space or parking to the need for a Performing Arts Complex for local productions.

Articulation of trellis reduces heat gain on the façade.

Collection of water demonstrates saving this important resource.

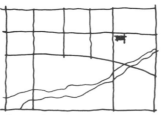

Project

Community

Region

5. Zoom In

Each planning and design component is part of a much larger whole. Green the details and you'll green the project.

Zoom In addresses many of the same issues as Zoom Out, but from a different perspective and on an entirely different scale. Zoom In is all about the details.

When you Zoom In, you undertake a careful analysis of the basic functional needs—how each building component works on its own and in conjunction with the greater whole—to create a balanced, holistic design solution.

Choosing a natural daylighting strategy, for example, means the project team must create different classroom proportions to maximize the daylighting and select design features to minimize the impact of glare on students, computer screens, and science equipment.

Zoom In details to consider include the nuances and interactions of each particular space, building programs, the building users, educational and teaching needs, utility and code regulations, district standards, and maintenance requirements.

Zoom In also addresses managerial issues, such as how the school supports the collaboration between the administration and faculty, teaching issues like integrating Career Tech completely into the curriculum, and financial issues such as funneling operating cost savings back to the school.

Zoom In is really a litmus test for a green school's master plan. Does this building material, or that architectural detail, reinforce the overall planning and design concept? Does it reinforce the Zoom Out and the Do Less principles? If not, then that building material or architectural detail is the wrong choice and the project team needs to find a different solution.

Understand the function and needs of the classroom learning environment.

Exterior shading device adds detail and interest to building façade.

6. Build Smart

Every planning and design choice should have a reason grounded in sustainability, every building or campus component should have a purpose, every detail should be necessary to the entire building or campus.

Perforated metal solar fins are integrated in the façade design.

Light shelves bounce daylight further into the classroom.

Operable windows allow teachers to control their own comfort, and are designed with mechanical "backup."

Skylight and clerestory windows allow light to be shared between floors—promoting daylight in the classroom.

When you Build Smart, sustainability and architecture are one and the same. There is no single design feature or component that you can point to and say, "That's the sustainable portion of the school." Sustainability and architecture are an integrated whole that cannot be divided one from the other.

How do you Build Smart? Choose the right site. Smart site selection assures the optimum building locations and orientation, which will help lower project costs, conserve open space, support a highly sustainable architectural design, and promote long-term operations savings.

When you Build Smart, nothing is superfluous. Everything is necessary. Every aspect of the site planning, building orientation, architectural design, building systems, and landscape architecture should work together in a seamless sustainable whole. Remove one element, and the entire sustainable system suffers. If someone insists that sunshades be removed from a building façade to save on upfront costs, for example, that decision will have an immediate and long-term negative impact on interior solar heat gain, HVAC use, and energy consumption and costs.

To Build Smart, use your money efficiently, spend it in the right places, do the right big gestures, and use measurement tools to validate those design and investment decisions. LPA, Inc. calls this "value architecture": spending the money where it will have the greatest impact.

Construction costs, for example, continue to rise. So, Build Smart. Simple building forms, an efficient structure, and elegant detailing will make the most of modest building materials, reducing the project's cost while creating a timeless building that is both unique and of its place.

To Build Smart, think simplicity not high tech. Natural ventilation, for example, starts with windows that open and close. There's not a whole lot of technology involved in that choice, but there are a lot of benefits, including less HVAC use and lower energy costs. Build Smart by designing a naturally ventilated school that has a back-up HVAC system rather than the other way around.

The simple tried and true solutions that for centuries guided planning and architecture prior to the advent of artificial lighting and HVAC systems are the keys to finding the best solutions when greening a school. To Build Smart, look for synergies with these time-honored principles, then marry those practices to appropriate sustainable technology options, to create affordable green solutions.

7. Enrich Lives

Green planning and design should enrich the lives of all the building users on a daily basis.

Design matters. Architectural beauty enriches the lives of everyone at the school, from students to staff, even visitors. And beauty has value that extends far beyond aesthetics.

Construct a school that's like a prison, and the students will act like prisoners.

A green school, however, honors and enriches the people who use it through beautiful design, a healthy indoor environment, abundant natural daylight and outdoor views, landscaping, and a carefully crafted and thoughtful site plan.

A green school Enriches Lives by providing a healthy environment that reduces the occurrence of illnesses. Healthy students, faculty, administrators, and staff, are happy students, faculty, administrators, and staff.

A green school Enriches Lives by generating a sense of community for students and staff. It is a place that a student is proud of and "owns." Thus, a green school has less truancy, less vandalism, and less trouble with surrounding residential neighborhoods.

Enrich Lives through "Campus Enrichment." Go beyond the physical facilities, building systems, and landscaping to enhance the educational programming through strategies like departmental relocation to improve function, efficiency, and collaboration.

Full-height operable doors and integrated louvers promote a naturally ventilated lobby.

Daylight enhances the natural stone, and provides a dramatic lobby entrance.

Beautiful green K–12 schools can Enrich Lives by restoring a sense of identity, place, and community to neighborhoods that may be struggling. And they do more.

Because green is embedded in the DNA of the school, that school becomes a powerful symbol of sustainability and environmental responsibility for the community.

Green schools Enrich Lives by educating students, teachers, administrators, and staff on a daily basis about sustainability, the environment, and the impact their choices and actions can have, for good or ill, on the environment.

Through this process, students, teachers, and staff, as well as school district administrators become champions of sustainability and the environment, which enriches all of our lives today and, more importantly, into the future.

8. Create Value

The green planning and design process should Create Value for all stakeholders.

Green schools aren't about added cost. They're about added *value*. Start using that mindset and you'll address new green school construction and green modernizations and expansions of existing schools differently.

Green schools, for example, Create Value, because they are flexible and adaptable to new educational needs, like Career Tech vocational training, which prepares high school students for well-paying jobs in their own communities. Skilled workers—who live, shop, work, raise families, and pay taxes in the communities in which they were raised and educated—make those communities more sustainable.

A green school Creates Value, because it won't cost more than a conventional school and it *will* have lower operating costs than a conventional school.

Skylights in the gymnasium allow lights to be off during the day.

Crystalline solar cell and glass canopy creates an aesthetically pleasing courtyard shading system.

Career technical education buildings can take advantage of photovoltaic systems, demonstrate scientific principles, and use the school as a teaching tool.

A green school Creates Value through its healthier indoor environment, fewer student and teacher illnesses, and lower absenteeism rates. Student educational and testing performance improves in green schools. Thus, green schools protect taxpayers' investment in education.

Green schools also Create Value by acting as a source of wealth. How?

Public school districts often find that the typical allowances or grants do not fully cover the cost of constructing a school today. LPA, Inc.'s 10 Sustainable Principles, however, help to lower the cost of construction by reinforcing the holistic and integrated construction and operation of a school in the 21st century.

In addition, local, state, and utility incentives, grants, and rebates for energy-efficient green features and technologies can provide some of the funds a district needs to construct a new green school or to implement the green modernization of an existing school.

In today's economic environment, school district officials must find a different way of doing business if they are going to balance the ever-increasing needs of students, teachers and their unions, test score requirements, and escalating utility and maintenance costs. Green schools are good business.

9. Prove It

Provide the hard numbers that all stakeholders—the school district, school administrators, faculty, maintenance staff, taxpayers, parents, and students—need about the true costs and benefits of green schools.

Most school district managers and staff and school administrators balk at the very idea of greening their schools, because they believe *Three Green School Myths:*

1. Green schools cost too much.

2. Green building and technology systems are much too sophisticated for school maintenance staff.

3. Green building materials aren't durable.

The truth is quite different.

The first myth is certainly the most pervasive. School stakeholders are far from the only people who believe that green costs much more than conventional buildings. *Sustainability Perceptions and Trends*, a joint January 2008 Jones Lang LaSalle and CoreNet Global international study, found that 90 percent of the more than 400 executives/respondents believed that constructing new high performance green buildings costs much more than constructing conventional buildings. Of those respondents, 30 percent believed green costs 5 to 10 percent more, and 22 percent believed green buildings were more than 10 percent more expensive to construct than comparable conventional buildings.

CHPS-designed school, Brea Olinda High School expansion building, matches existing campus of tilt-up concrete.

In *Building Design+Construction's* October 2007 Green Buildings Research White Paper, 78 percent of the *architecture, engineering, and construction* respondents believed that going green "Adds significantly to first costs."

Perception, however, is not reality.

As discussed in Chapter 2, new green buildings cost the same as—and in some cases less than—comparable conventional schools. Prove It to your stakeholders with Davis Langdon's *Cost of Green Revisited* 2007 study, which found that "there is no significant difference in average costs for green buildings as compared to non-green buildings ... Average construction costs have risen dramatically the past three years—between 25% and 30%. And yet we still see a large number of projects achieving LEED [certification] within budget."

Prove It with this book. Every new school, building, modernization, and expansion project in this book was completed within the parameters of the school district's or State of California's budget requirements.

As for the second myth, green building and technology systems are no more complex—and often are less complex—than conventional systems. Besides, part of the green post-construction process includes education and training for operations and maintenance staff to assure optimum performance of green building and technology systems.

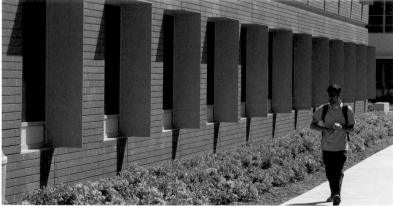

Sunscreens protect glazing from heat gain on west façade.

Finally, green building materials are just as durable as conventional materials. Steel with recycled content—even 100 percent recycled content—is just as strong as traditionally manufactured steel, and it is being used confidently in major buildings around the world. Low- and zero-VOC paints last just as long as conventional paints.

As these *Three Green School Myths* demonstrate, stakeholders require quantifiable, verifiable performance measurement of their green schools. And we have the tools now to do that. With software programs like Eco-Tech and Revit, for example, design decisions are based on actual performance data.

The simple truth is that green schools make financial sense. Prove It by tracking a green school's reduced energy and water consumption, lower operating and maintenance costs, and teachers' fewer sick days and greater job satisfaction. Often, teachers quit schools with unhealthy indoor environments, unattractive work environments, and low job satisfaction. What is the cost to the school district to replace a teacher?

Because green schools have healthy indoor environments, *students* have fewer sick days and are happier to go to school, which means lower student absenteeism rates and higher ADA rates, as well as higher test scores.

When you prove the true costs and benefits of green schools, parents often choose to buy homes in neighborhoods with green schools, which raises property values and that brings more tax revenues into the school district. For private schools, green is a way to brand the school and recruit new students.

When you prove the true costs and benefits of green schools, they become more attractive to community residents who *don't* have children, because green schools raise their property values, which enhances their investment in their homes. These residents are much more inclined to vote for more school bonds to construct more green schools and carry out green modernizations and expansions of existing schools.

Steel canopy defines entrance, provides shade, is durable, and qualifies for recycled content.

Steel sunscreens scale openings for younger children, and reduce heat gain on building façades.

Exterior walkways reduce building energy usage and provide unique opportunities to articulate the building façade.

10. Step Up

Stop talking about it and start doing it. The time for green schools is now.

Too many school districts are ignoring green schools, or taking a "wait and see" attitude, rather than Stepping Up and greening their schools.

Why aren't they Stepping Up? The most common excuses are:

- It costs more. (Not true.)

- It's too complicated to do. (Not true. CHPS and LEED provide clear guidelines, and the green planning and design process essentially removes one whole step from conventional construction—Value Engineering.)

- I have to pass a school board resolution. (Not necessarily. Start with one project and build on that success.)

The seamless addition to the campus of a high performance building demonstrates how a green facility can fit the existing context.

Durable materials of concrete and CMU (concrete block) minimize long-term operational and maintenance costs.

Not only are school districts running out of excuses to not Step Up, they're running into more and more demands *to* Step Up.

Students are demanding green. Schools are now filling with a generation of students who are being raised on sustainability and environmental awareness and they expect their schools to be green.

Parents are demanding green. They assume—based on what they see on TV, hear on the radio, read in newspapers and magazines, and find on the Internet—that their local institutions, including their schools, are green or are going green, because sustainability enhances their children's health and learning, it's just good common sense, and it's a sensible use of their tax dollars. A school district that has to constantly explain to increasingly irate parents that it has not adopted a green building and renovation program is a school district that is going to face increasingly vociferous demands that it take action now.

Do you want to lead or follow? Many school district administrators say "I don't want to be on the cutting-edge."

But green buildings aren't cutting edge.

Sustainability and green building principles have been around for centuries. California's Spanish missions constructed in the 18th and 19th centuries, for example, are the epitome of sustainability, as are the mid-20th century "finger plan" schools that maximize natural ventilation and daylighting. The U.S. green building movement of the last decade has simply taken historic sustainability principles and recast them for modern needs.

Green schools enable you to be a leader without taking a risk.

So, what are you going to do? Green schools are not a fad, they make sense, and dollars and cents, they're the right thing to do, students, parents, and teachers want them, and more and more cities are mandating them.

If someone asks you today what you are going to do to create a sustainable environment, how are you going to answer them?

Lessons in Sustainable Planning and Design

The many planning, design, technology, and other strategies to green a new or existing school are too numerous to list in a single book, and they are growing exponentially on a daily basis.

The following are just some of the basic, cost-effective sustainable planning and design strategies that LPA, Inc. has learned by applying its 10 Sustainable Principles to every kind of school, institutional, commercial, and residential building.

Landscape architecture

Landscape architecture is one of the most important and cost-effective tools for creating a green building or a green campus. Trees, flowers, shrubs, hedges, and native grasses cost far less than the mechanical systems, building materials, and infrastructure that, in the past, were used to cool and insulate buildings and mitigate stormwater runoff.

First, landscape architecture can significantly reduce heat islands, which will lower HVAC requirements and costs. Heat islands are asphalt and other dark, non-reflective surfaces on roofs, walkways, roads, and parking lots that absorb and slowly release solar heat throughout the day and into the night, which can raise surrounding temperatures by as much as 10 degrees. Heat islands make buildings hotter, which means greater air conditioning use and energy consumption.

A green screen—a metal lattice planted with vines and/or climbing flowers—along a building's western façade, for example, will mitigate that heat island and limit interior heat absorption. Placing trees along the south façade of a building will provide both shade and heat reduction in the summer. By selecting deciduous trees that drop their leaves every autumn, the building will enjoy warmth and sunlight during the cold winter months, which will reduce heating and artificial lighting usage and lower energy bills.

Trees and arbors planted around (and throughout) a surface parking lot minimize heat islands and create a shaded, attractive, even welcoming parking area.

Second, select drought-tolerant and native plants for the landscape architecture plan. Once these plants are established, they'll need little (if any) irrigation, which will conserve water. They'll also need very little maintenance, which will reduce the school's long-term operating costs.

Greenscreens reduce heat gain and create a softer and more welcoming façade.

Native drought-tolerant landscape requires less water and reduces maintenance costs.

Bioswales integrated into passive open space, provide a safe learning opportunity for students.

Field subdrainage systems address stormwater management strategies, providing a high level of playability for athletic teams.

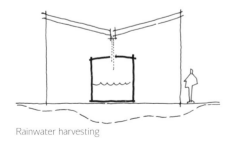
Rainwater harvesting

Library reading room looks over green roof, providing a strong visual link to green design strategy.

Third, landscape architecture can also manage stormwater runoff, which carries automobile contaminants from roadways and parking lots into waterways and can also lead to flooding. Strategies like bioswales—landscaped trenches or small canals that are lined with grass and plants—clean, slow, and reduce the amount of stormwater runoff from the site, while also beautifying the school.

Fourth, landscape architecture can be used to buffer noise and to screen visually unattractive items such as mechanical systems and dumpsters.

Water conservation and stormwater management
Water-conserving plumbing fixtures can save tens of thousands of gallons of potable water annually.

Outside, drought-tolerant and native plants also conserve water. Install a low-consumption drip irrigation system that uses recycled rather than potable water.

An increasingly popular strategy is an Internet-based landscape irrigation system linked to weather satellites that adjusts the timing and amount of irrigation according to current weather conditions, including air temperature, precipitation, wind, and humidity.

Stormwater management strategies start with landscape architecture and open space, which can minimize—or even eliminate—the need for traditional stormwater management infrastructure, and that helps to reduce the school's overall construction and operating costs. How?

Open space in and of itself absorbs a good deal of stormwater.

In addition, bioswales, natural and man-made wetlands, natural and man-made detention ponds, even a green (landscaped) roof all help to slow, cleanse, and store stormwater runoff, minimizing erosion, pollution, and flood risks.

The plants of a green roof, for example, absorb and store rain, reducing runoff, and they also filter pollutants from rain and stormwater runoff.

Energy and atmosphere
In the U.S., buildings consume 39 percent of the nation's total annual energy supply and generate 48 percent of the country's carbon dioxide emissions.

Green design strategies and technologies reduce energy consumption by 20 percent to 50 percent or more compared to a conventional building, and that significantly reduces greenhouse gas emissions and energy costs.

Insulation—which keeps hot air out and cool air in during the summer, and cold air out and warm air in during the winter—is a simple and vital means of conserving energy. Insulation starts with framing. A 2x4 framed wall, for example, will have an insulating value of R13 using conventional fiberglass batt insulation. A 2x6 framed wall, however, accommodates R19 insulation, which provides 50 percent more insulation than R13.

The kind of insulation chosen for a green building is also critical. Conventional insulation often has toxins that can leak into the indoor environment. Green choices such as soybean-based insulation or cotton insulation, however, do not have these toxins while providing excellent building insulation.

A green roof also provides significant insulation that reduces the amount of heat that penetrates into the building interior, keeping the building cooler in summer, which lowers upfront air conditioning requirements and reduces long-term energy consumption. A green roof keeps the building interior warmer in winter by reducing the amount of heat loss, which lowers initial heating requirements and reduces long-term energy consumption.

A green roof also significantly reduces—and sometimes eliminates—the rooftop heat island effect by absorbing solar heat, which further reduces a building's air conditioning requirements and upfront costs, lowering energy consumption.

The lighting system is responsible for between 25 and 44 percent of an entire building's energy consumption. A building with abundant natural daylighting will need less artificial lighting, and it will use that artificial lighting system less, greatly reducing energy consumption.

Of course, an artificial lighting system is still important. Indirect lighting systems, advanced fluorescent lamps and ballasts, compact fluorescent lamps, Light Emitting Diodes (LEDs), High Intensity Discharge (HID), and other lighting technologies all use significantly less energy than conventional lighting systems and components.

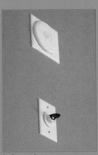

Natural cotton fiber insulation made from recycled jeans.

Infrared occupancy sensor and photo cell.

Security sensor.

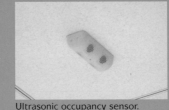

Ultrasonic occupancy sensor.

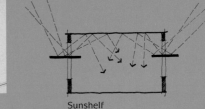

Sunshelf

Large expanses of flat roofs on gymnasiums and classroom buildings become excellent locations for photovoltaic installations.

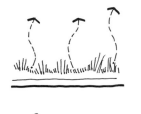
Greenroof

Broken concrete from the original demolished slab is reused to create an "outdoor collaboration room."

Low-maintenance epoxy coating on floor and synthetic turf "carpet" explore creative green strategies in student collaborative area.

Install occupancy and daylight sensors and controls to reduce artificial lighting use according to the amount of daylight in a space and whether or not a space is occupied to save even more energy.

The HVAC system should be energy efficient and it should not use ozone-depleting hydrochlorofluorocarbon (HCFC), Halon, or chlorofluorocarbon (CFC)-based refrigerants.

When it comes to energy-conservation strategies, one of the most effective tools is an energy meter. Meter everything that uses energy, from the HVAC system on down to computers. Metering and monitoring energy-consuming equipment and building systems immediately raises a red flag whenever a boiler or a computer is not performing at optimal energy efficiency, enabling the facility manager to make any necessary programming or technology adjustments to maintain energy conservation standards and keep operating costs down.

Renewable energy technologies include natural gas fuel cells. Geothermal systems draw heat from the earth to warm a building and expel heat into the earth to cool a building. Biomass systems burn biological wastes— everything from agricultural debris and weeds to manure and sewage sludge—rather than coal or oil to generate electricity.

Photovoltaic systems are becoming more commonplace. These systems can be anything from rooftop panels to panels that shade surface parking lots, and solar technologies imbedded into the building façade, even the windows.

School districts can also purchase Renewable Energy Credits from utility companies and other vendors to assure that a school is powered by renewable energy sources rather than oil and coal.

Materials and resources
The project team can significantly enhance a school's sustainability by using a wide variety of green building materials that promote a healthy indoor environment and have minimal negative impact on the world's natural resources.

When constructing a building on a previously developed site, the team can conserve resources by reusing the existing building shell and even some of the interior elements. Concrete from a demolished building can be reused in sidewalks, roadways, and plazas and courtyards.

Vital green building materials include low- and zero-VOC (Volatile Organic Compound) paints, sealants, and adhesives that don't off-gas the toxins found in their conventional counterparts.

Green flooring choices include natural fiber and recycled carpeting, natural linoleum made, for example, from jute and linseed oil, FSC (Forest Stewardship Certified) wood products, and rapidly renewable resources like bamboo, as well as strawboard made from wheat (as opposed to often formaldehyde-laced particle board), all of which are priced comparably to conventional materials and support a healthier indoor air quality.

Building materials with recycled content are manufactured using less energy and fewer natural resources than conventional materials, which makes them particularly important to a green building. New steel frames, for example, have a minimum of 28 percent recycled steel content, and often 60 percent or more.

Other common building materials with recycled content include acoustic ceiling tiles, carpeting, paneling, signage, and even furniture.

Materials should also be selected based on their recyclability at the end of their useful lives.

Purchase building materials from within a 500-mile radius of the project site. Not only will this earn the building LEED points and support the local economy, it will also lower energy consumption and greenhouse gas emissions and reduce the project's costs, because the materials are being shipped over a shorter (less expensive) distance.

Finally, a green project team should assure that at least 50 percent, and preferably 75 percent or more, of the construction waste is reused on site or recycled, rather than sent to landfills.

Indoor environmental quality planning and design

Key to a superior quality indoor environment are:

- Abundant natural daylighting

- Abundant outdoor views

- Fresh filtered air.

Countertop made from recycled glass and concrete offers a durable and sustainable alternative.

Sunshades protect the two-story lobby glazing.

Integrate structure and mechanical to maximize natural light.

1. A building structure that supports lower floor-to-floor heights—which reduces the amount of building materials needed and the consumption of natural resources—while maximizing the interior volume.

2. Natural ventilation with mechanical back-up.

3. Planning, design, and construction strategies that reduce the consumption of natural resources by requiring fewer building materials, like reducing the number of "finishes" in a project by exposing the structure or floor slabs.

4. Integrating the curriculum and programming into the school design.

5. An integrated planning and design project team that includes the school district, school administrators, and users who base their decisions on sustainability principles.

A building's shape can go a long way toward making it green and creating a superior indoor environment. A narrow building, for example, supports both natural daylighting and natural ventilation strategies. So does a circular or cylindrical design. (Both strategies also help to reduce a building's development footprint.)

Strategies for abundant natural daylighting include large windows with Low Emission (Low-E) glazing, atriums, clerestories, skylights, light monitors, lightshelves, and glass curtainwalls.

Good indoor air quality (IAQ) starts by limiting pollutant sources. Thus, a construction IAQ management plan and the use of low-emitting building materials and furnishings are critical.

Provide separate exhaust systems for copier rooms and janitorial closets to protect indoor air quality.

Carbon dioxide monitors automatically keep indoor fresh air levels at pre-determined limits. Air filters throughout the HVAC system can make the indoor air cleaner and healthier than the outdoor air. Ultraviolet emitters (UVC) in the HVAC system prevent the growth of micro-organisms and mold caused by humidity and standing water at the cooling coils.

A natural ventilation system will go a long way toward assuring superior indoor environmental quality. Several strategies support a natural ventilation system, from building orientation and shape to operable windows, double curtainwalls, and wind chimneys.

A double curtainwall system has a façade of two separate panes of glass separated by a 30-inch air space, which not only brings natural daylight into the building and gives users spectacular outdoor views, it also vents heat out the top of the building, and on cold days it captures warm air to help heat the building.

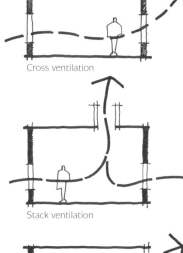

Cross ventilation

Stack ventilation

Combination

Operable windows maximize thermal comfort of occupants.

Wind chimneys have been used for centuries from the American Southwest to the Middle East and India for natural ventilation of a building interior. A wind chimney can be as simple as a rooftop chimney designed to use temperature and pressure differentials to drive clean fresh air into and through a building. A wind chimney can also be a more complex system, like a tower sunk from three to several feet into the ground and attached to a building that draws cool air up from the earth (which has a stable, cooler temperature than above-surface air) and into the building. When it is cold outside at night, this wind chimney system draws air up from the earth that warms the building floors.

Temperature is a critical component of indoor environmental quality. A growing number of energy-efficient heating and cooling technologies are helping buildings become more sustainable while making occupants more comfortable, starting with underfloor air distribution systems, which deliver conditioned air at a lower velocity just above floor level. The conditioned air rises naturally and disperses throughout the space. This delivery system uses lower fan pressure and speeds, and therefore less energy, than conventional HVAC systems.

An inexpensive and energy-efficient HVAC strategy is night flushing, which uses a system of fans and vents to push warm interior air out of a building at night and draw in the cooler evening air, which delays heat gain during the day, and that reduces the cooling load. Night flushing also helps to keep the indoor air fresh by ejecting stale air.

Maintaining good indoor air quality requires proactive building operations plans, including cleaning procedures, the use of low- and zero-VOC cleaning products, and regular maintenance and monitoring of the HVAC system.

Exterior design

A green building does not simply sprout from the ground and rise up to the sky. It *connects to* the ground, and the sky, and the weather, and the surrounding uses with a mix of exterior elements that enhance the sustainability and function of the building.

Façade design

Building orientation will directly affect building design. In warmer climates, a building with a northern orientation, for example, can have a more open façade to bring in natural daylight, which reduces artificial lighting and air conditioning use and costs. The southern façade is given

HVAC fabric air diffuser.

Honeycomb Solera® glazing panels used above, and light shelves diffuse and project light further into classroom.

Steel louvers protect glazing from heat gain, reducing the mechanical load on the building.

Louvers promote warmer air at slower velocity to ventilate the gymnasium.

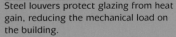
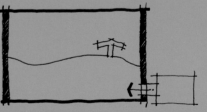
Displacement ventilation

Step Up: 10 actions

Here's what you can do right now to start greening your schools.

1. If you're a parent: don't assume. Pick up the phone. Call your school district. Ask questions.

2. If you're a school district: pick up the phone. Learn about the many different funding sources available to you that support new green school construction and green modernizations and expansions of existing schools.

3. Pass a resolution mandating green schools for your district.

4. Enact energy and water savings standards for the schools in your district.

5. Integrate the school's curriculum with national sustainability principles to create a "hands on" learning environment.

6. Mandate healthy teaching environments in your district.

7. Market your green school to strengthen its "brand" and educate the community about how, in conjunction with its curriculum, your green school has greater value in the community.

8. Involve the students. Initiate a school-wide recycling program. Have student teams evaluate the school's energy usage as class projects. Create student advocacy programs to ensure that green policies are followed during the school day.

9. Require that your maintenance staff use green cleaning products and processes.

10. Buy local to reduce the packaging, cost, and greenhouse gas emissions of shipping your furniture, fixtures, and equipment purchases.

Step Up and take these actions and you'll be leading the way on green schools without risk.

Building green for future generations.

exterior shading devices to minimize solar heat gain, which reduces air conditioning requirements. Strategies can include architectural elements such as overhangs and exterior sunshades, as well as landscape architecture like green screens that both shade and insulate walls.

A western façade, which gets all of the afternoon sun, acts as a heat island. For buildings in warm climates, shade the western façade with landscape architecture such as trees or green screens, or with a canopy or arcade, or with sunshades. Windows and doors should be kept to a minimum—or eliminated entirely—on a western façade to avoid interior solar heat gain.

Thermal lag and the diurnal differential

In desert regions like the American Southwest and southern California, the project team can create a less costly passive design—thermal lag— that makes use of the diurnal differential (a swing in temperatures of 25 degrees or more between day and night) to help cool a school building. Design strategies can range from the use of traditional adobe to solar walls made from perforated metal with a 12-inch air space between the wall and the building structure. Solar walls function the same way as the thick mass of an adobe wall. The air space between the wall and the building structure preheats air for the heating system in the winter, saving energy. In the summer, the solar wall reduces interior heat gain by venting hot air up and away from the building, keeping the interior cooler, which reduces air conditioning use.

The roof

A conventional roof is just one big heat island. But it doesn't have to be. A light-colored Energy Star roof, for example, reflects solar heat away from the building, keeping roof and building interior temperatures significantly cooler.

A valuable multipurpose strategy—especially for city and suburban school projects with constrained sites and limited open space opportunities—is a green (landscaped) roof planted with hardy, drought-tolerant shrubs, flowers, grasses, and ground cover. A green roof has many benefits, all of which lower project costs and make the building more sustainable.

Whether the building has an Energy Star or a green roof, it should also have a rooftop rainwater collection system to support the school's landscape irrigation and plumbing systems and to reduce utility-provided water consumption.

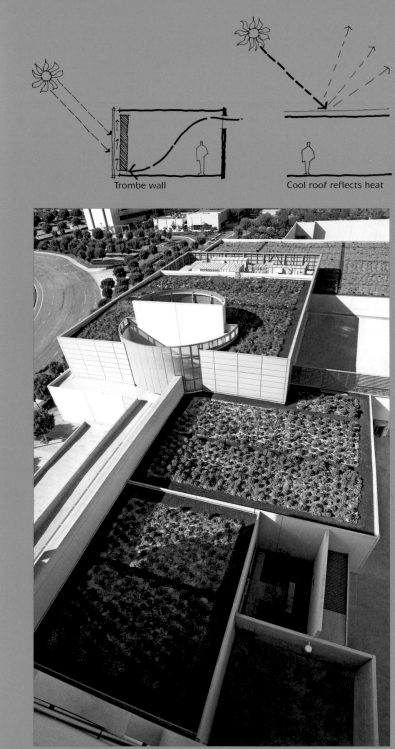

Trombe wall

Cool roof reflects heat

Green roof with drought-tolerant planting.

CHAPTER 5

Cesar Chavez Elementary School

Long Beach, California
2004

On September 18, 2004, one of the first truly green K–12 schools in California opened to its first students: the $15 million low-rise 75,000-square-foot Cesar Chavez Elementary School, a Kindergarten through Fifth Grade school designed for 830 children in downtown Long Beach.

From its inception, this school has been a living laboratory, educating the city, the school district, the surrounding neighborhoods, and its students, faculty, and administrators about the natural environment and the benefits of a green school that cost no more than a comparable conventional school.

Cesar Chavez Elementary School has also helped ease overcrowding in nearby schools, thereby reducing student busing in the district, and it alleviated the need for year-round school schedules in the district.

The school has won numerous design awards from organizations including Orange County AIA, the South Bay AIA, CEFPI/AIA, CHPS, and C.A.S.H.—proving that a green educational facility can be functional and aesthetically pleasing.

In 2005, the school also won an AIA California Council-Public Utility Savings By Design Merit Award. The jurors wrote: "The ability to integrate innovative environmental technologies into a well-sculpted building is a tough job and done extremely well in this project."

Planning a model green elementary school

Back in 2000, the City of Long Beach and the Long Beach Unified School District each had problems that could be solved if they worked together.

The City had two disparate and adjacent neighborhoods on very different tracks: the newer and more affluent World Trade Center downtown business district and an older, moderate-income residential neighborhood that had been declining in recent years. The City had embarked on a redevelopment program, but it needed something to tie the two neighborhoods together, help further the revitalization of the residential neighborhood, and provide a gateway to the downtown district.

At the same time, the Long Beach Unified School District (LBUSD) was struggling with overcrowded elementary schools in this area, the high costs of busing, and the prospect of being forced to adopt year-round school schedules to meet the educational needs of this community. The district also wanted to explore green school design options.

The City and the LBUSD solved their problems on a 2.6-acre site at the northwest corner of West Broadway and Golden Avenue, three blocks north of the Pacific Ocean, between and adjacent to the World Trade Center business district and the older residential neighborhood in downtown Long Beach.

The City kicked things off by constructing Cesar E. Chavez Park, a new 7-acre neighborhood park adjacent to the 2.6-acre site to help further the renaissance of the adjacent residential neighborhood.

Keeping its municipal partner in mind, the LBUSD had several objectives for the new Cesar Chavez Elementary School that it would build on the adjacent 2.6-acre site. The district wanted to:

- Build a catalyst for the revival of this downtown district, using architecture and landscape architecture to unite the adjacent residential neighborhood and the adjacent business district, creating a gateway for these rapidly redeveloping downtown areas and a more pedestrian-friendly public realm.
- Showcase intelligent, environmentally responsible, sustainable building design for a municipal school.
- Change the existing institutional nature of recent city school projects into a welcoming environment for 830 children.

The LBUSD financed the development of Cesar Chavez Elementary School with funds from its new construction budget. Because Cesar Chavez Elementary School is a joint-use facility shared with the city's Parks and Recreation Department—which uses the gymnasium building and other recreational facilities during off-school hours—that Department provided some funding to help construct the school. The LBUSD also offset some of the costs of the $15-million project using two different programs:

Savings By Design: This program—sponsored by four of California's largest utilities under the auspices of the Public Utilities Commission—encourages high-performance non-residential building design and construction by providing a range of services, including owner incentives to help offset the costs of energy-efficient building features.

Proposition 47: California's Proposition 47 Energy Allowance Grant specifically targeted new school facilities. Cesar Chavez Elementary was the first K–12 school in California to make use of Proposition 47.

The LBUSD broke ground on Cesar Chavez Elementary in Spring 2003, and the school was completed in September 2004.

LPA, Inc.'s multi-purpose architectural design

The 2.6-acre campus has 34 classrooms, including a special education classroom, a gymnasium that also serves as a multi-purpose room for the community after hours and on weekends, administration offices, a library, a computer learning center, and a separate kindergarten playground.

A covered lunch shelter provides both protection from the elements and abundant natural light. A portion of the adjacent Cesar E. Chavez Park is closed off for student activities during the school day.

LPA, Inc's design of the low-rise architecture is playful and welcoming. The administration/gymnasium building, which faces the adjacent residential neighborhood, has sweeping, curving lines that are welcoming to the community. The classroom buildings, which border the World Trade Center downtown business district, have clean, horizontal lines, more in keeping with that adjacent commercial district.

The design of the three two-story main buildings reflects, symbolizes, and unites the disparate adjoining districts. The buildings' burnished concrete block base is nearly maintenance free and vandal resistant.

Green features

Several green strategies shaped the functional and aesthetic design of the school. Aside from the central plant, which the school district requested, none of the green features cost any more than their conventional components, and all of them help to reduce the school's annual operating costs.

Site planning and building orientation

The school was carefully sited on the 2.6-acre property to give it an ideal orientation that reaps the greatest benefits from the sun and wind. The main façades, for example, face north and south. The north façade has many large windows that bring natural daylight into the school, while the south façade has a variety of shading features to keep out sun heat and glare. The orientation, just three blocks from the Pacific Ocean, also enhances the school's natural ventilation system.

Natural daylighting and artificial lighting

Natural daylight fills the classrooms, gymnasium, offices, and public spaces. Operable northern windows with Low-E laminated glazing in the classrooms and public areas bring in daylight. Natural daylighting is also filtered through a series of lightshelves and sunscreens, as well as light monitors in the roof that bring northern light into the public areas, including the corridors. (Windows on the east and west exposures were kept to a minimum and sunshades were used when necessary.) The lunch shelter has a series of linear saw-toothed skylights that bring in natural light.

A dimming system in the classrooms, offices, and public areas automatically dims or shuts down the indirect and direct T8 fluorescent lighting when sufficient daylighting is present, which saves electricity. This was the first use of indirect school lighting in the LBUSD's history. Occupancy sensors shut off lighting when no one is present in a room, further saving electricity.

Heat mitigation

Low-E glazing on all of Cesar Chavez Elementary's windows stops the direct transmission of heat, but not sunlight.

Horizontal screening with sunscreens, canopies, and shading on the southern façade also block solar heat gain and lower HVAC costs.

Trees planted along the south, west, and east façades of the school buildings—which have the greatest amount of sun exposure—provide natural shading and filtered light.

Trees planted between the parking court and the northern side of the school, and trees planted around the perimeter and along the bordering streets, help to shade the campus and reduce the number and intensity of heat islands.

Rather than heat-absorbing AC paving, concrete was used for the school's main drive aisle and on the hard courts. The higher reflective value of the concrete helps to reduce heat gain by as much as 50 percent.

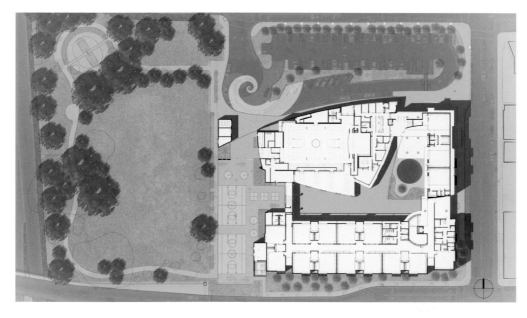

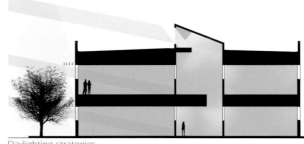

Daylighting strategies.

HVAC

A central water-cooled HVAC plant with four-pipe fan coil units provides greater efficiency, lower costs, and ease of maintenance compared to a package unit system. While initially more expensive than a package unit system, the plant will provide long-term cost savings through lower energy and maintenance costs.

Cesar Chavez Elementary School was also oriented to provide natural ventilation, created by a series of operable clerestories and windows that provide great cross-ventilation and cool the classrooms. Operable skylights vent air from the common areas. Light monitors in the roof also conduct heat out of the school. This system significantly reduces HVAC needs and costs.

A living laboratory

The students are learning about and experiencing the natural environment on a daily, practical basis by studying in natural daylight rather than under artificial lighting, breathing fresh air rather than recycled air, walking to and from school on tree-shaded sidewalks, and contributing paper, plastic, and aluminum to the recycling bins in their classrooms.

The surrounding community is learning about the power of the natural environment as they see the almost-daily changes made to their neighborhoods and their lives by the enhanced public realm and a school facility that has raised the bar for the entire area.

The LBUSD is learning the many benefits of green design for students, teachers, and administrators, and it is seeing the lower energy and water consumption and costs generated by that green design.

Outcome

LPA, Inc.'s design was intended to reduce energy usage and costs by 33 percent more than is required by the California Title 24 energy code, which is the strictest in the nation. Actually, it reduced energy consumption by 68 percent compared to a similar but conventional school: an 8 percent reduction in electricity, and a 60 percent reduction in natural gas use.

The school's water conservation systems were supposed to reduce runoff and irrigation and domestic water use by as much as 30 percent. Actually, Cesar Chavez Elementary uses 58 percent less water than a comparable conventional school.

Prior to the school's opening, 1,800 neighborhood children were bused daily to area schools. Now, more than 500 students are no longer bused to other schools. Indeed, many children now walk or ride their bicycles to Cesar Chavez Elementary School, which saves fuel and reduces air pollution generated by the school district's buses. The surrounding community benefits, too, because of the joint use of the gymnasium and playfields, as well as the inclusion of a community wellness clinic into the school program.

The school's benefits extend beyond the immediate community. The City of Long Beach considers Cesar Chavez Elementary School to be the cornerstone for the future of the adjacent redeveloping residential district and the World Trade Center downtown business district.

The LBUSD considers Cesar Chavez Elementary School a great success for its students and teachers, and for the surrounding community.

Of particular importance, because of this school's success, the LBUSD hired LPA, Inc. in 2006 to create a district-wide facilities master plan that uses Cesar Chavez Elementary as a model of sustainable design for all future school projects built in the district.

CHAPTER 6

Beverly Hills High School Science & Technology Center

**Beverly Hills, California
2007**

Famed Beverly Hills High School (BHHS) was founded in 1927. It has a current enrollment of more than 2,400 students. Its original architect, Robert F. Farquhar, used a French Normandy architectural style for the two-story campus buildings with off-white stucco, several towers, terra cotta roof tiles, courtyards, and extensive landscaping.

Surprisingly, the BHHS zip code isn't 90210. It's 90212. The TV series *Beverly Hills 90210*'s creator, Aaron Spelling, whose daughter Tori attended BHHS, chose to create a fictitious West Beverly Hills High School with the bogus zip code, rather than use the actual school on which the series was based. Other celebrities who attended BHHS prior to gaining fame include future actors Carrie Fisher, Angelina Jolie, and Nicholas Cage.

Beyond its celebrity, BHHS has a rigorous college prep curriculum and two common problems facing many older schools: obsolescent buildings at the end of their useful lives and limited space on which to construct necessary state-of-the-art facilities for its students.

Project goals

BHHS needed a new math, science, and technology building.

The Beverly Hills High School District, BHHS administrators, and faculty, however, wanted much more than just a new building. They wanted the new facility to have state-of-the-art classrooms and educational development facilities that would serve teachers, students, and the community. They wanted to showcase science and technology to the community, giving the historic school a forward-looking facility and image.

They wanted a new "gateway" building: a new front door for the north end of the school that provided a clear connection between the pastoral campus and adjacent high-rise Century City.

Finally, they wanted the new building to be green.

All on a one-acre site.

LPA, Inc. was hired, first to provide program and study design concepts for the new building, and later to provide comprehensive design services, including architecture, interior design, graphics, and landscape architecture.

Throughout the 2002–2004 collaborative design phase, the greatest challenge LPA, Inc. and the district faced was rapidly escalating construction labor and materials costs, which led LPA, Inc. to employ significant value engineering measures to mitigate the cost increases as much as possible, without compromising quality or efficiency.

Construction began in January 2006, and the building was completed in September 2007.

Program

In collaboration with a committee of BHHS faculty and administrators and school district staff, LPA, Inc. created a four-story L-shaped 78,000-square-foot building with 18 math classrooms, 11 science labs, a computer lab, a 100-seat lecture hall, faculty work areas, and a multi-purpose educational development center for teacher training, testing, program development, collaboration, staff mentoring and teaming, and community outreach.

Each floor of the new building connects directly to the classroom floors of an adjacent four-story academic building constructed in the 1960s.

The program also included a new courtyard between the science and technology center and the adjacent existing classroom building that continues the courtyard plan of the original campus.

Architectural design

LPA, Inc. had to create an architectural design that would integrate the new science and technology center into the original campus and complement the adjacent four-story classroom building constructed in the 1960s. LPA, Inc. also had to create a visual connection to adjacent high-rise Century City and use design to reflect the purpose of the new building and to inspire students and faculty alike.

To fit the necessary programming onto the small site and maintain the campus' emphasis on outdoor space, LPA, Inc. created an L-shaped building design that, by rising four stories, provided the necessary square footage and a new courtyard that showcases science and acts as a teaching tool. A white tower on the northeast corner of the building visually connects the new building to other towers on campus, and to the much taller office towers of Century City.

Tessellations—repeated, interlocking shapes found in nature, science, and math—were used throughout the architecture and landscape architecture design to both reflect the uses of the new building and to further integrate the building into the existing campus. The courtyard, for example, has a tessellated paving pattern incorporated into a Fibonacci spiral (a series where each number is a function of the preceding two numbers), which is also reflected in the acorns of the oak tree in the center of the courtyard. From the fourth floor, students can look down and view the tessellation series used throughout the entire courtyard.

Built-in seating along the south-facing lobby windows on the second, third, and fourth floors encourage socialization and enjoyment of the outdoor views.

A major teaching tool is the main-floor lobby's graphic walls: a prominent mural using portraits, photographs, and drawings, everything from a portrait of Galileo to a picture of the moon rover, showcasing a particular subject covered in the science and technology center. In addition, a 150-foot-long "science timeline" displays each of the biological, physical chemical, and life sciences covered in the school's curriculum.

Fun facts are integrated into each of the graphic walls to make students aware of the simple things in their lives that have an impact on the environment. Oak tree and acorn images are featured prominently on the graphic walls to tie the interior to the exterior courtyard and to continue the tessellation theme.

Green features

While the Beverly Hills School District chose not to pursue either CHPS or LEED ratings for the BHHS science and technology center, LPA, Inc. incorporated criteria from both programs into the building's planning and design.

Heat island and solar heat gain mitigation

The constrained site prohibited optimal building orientation, so LPA, Inc. made the best of those conditions. The west side of the building, for example, was given relatively few windows to minimize significant interior solar heat gain. While half of the classrooms face west, that side of the building lies within the shadow of Century City office towers, which mitigates the heat island effect. Similarly, the east façade is shaded somewhat by adjacent existing school buildings.

The Center is topped with an Energy Star "cool roof" that reflects solar heat away from the building. The south façade has a series of sunshades to prevent interior solar heat gain. Southern, western, and eastern windows have PPG Solexia insulated Low-E glazing. Landscaping was used to provide additional heat island mitigation (see below).

In the main courtyard, a large oak tree provides shade, helping to mitigate the heat island effect. A majority of the concrete paving is natural gray, which has high reflectivity, further reducing heat gain.

Natural daylighting

The lobbies—the main corridors—of each floor face south. The south-facing 8-foot-tall lobby windows have light shelves to help bring additional natural daylighting into the interior with solar heat gain mitigated by clip-on solar shades. In the classrooms, which have 11-foot ceilings, the lower 3 feet of the south-facing walls are solid and the window glazing rises from 3 to 11 feet, thereby maximizing the performance of the light shelves, while minimizing heat gain.

Artificial lighting

The classroom, science lab, and lecture hall artificial lighting system is a combination of energy-efficient direct and indirect T-8 pendant lighting, motion sensors, and stepped daylight controls that reduce the artificial light from 100 percent, to 67 percent, to 33 percent, and then off based on the natural daylighting light levels.

This lighting system consumes 55 percent less energy than a comparable conventional system that meets minimum energy code requirements.

HVAC

The science and technology center is connected to BHHS's central plant, which is controlled by energy-efficient variable-air volume boxes and an Energy Management System. Recognizing the value of having this sophisticated system commissioned to ensure that it performed as designed, an important strategy in assuring optimum energy efficiency, the school district and the project team hired an independent consultant commissioning agent who guaranteed that the system was installed and performing as planned.

Energy conservation and generation

Many of the strategies discussed above—from the Energy Star roof to the use of natural daylighting, high-performance insulated window glazing, T-8 light fixtures, and heat island mitigation—help the science and technology center to conserve energy by reducing air conditioning and artificial lighting use.

In addition, the tower was designed to support a future steel canopy with photovoltaic panels that will generate some of the electricity the school needs, provide an additional teaching tool, and serve as an appropriate landmark for a 21st-century school.

Water conservation and stormwater management

The science and technology center's plumbing fixtures meet the water-conservation requirements of the Energy Policy Act of 1992 and include ultra low-flow lavatories that have a 0.5 gallon per minute (GPM) flow rate, which is 80 percent below the 2.5 GPM baseline standard.

Daylighting strategies.

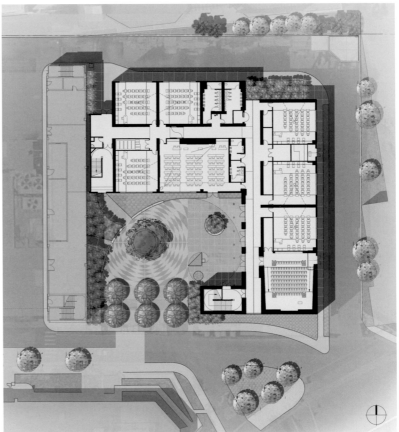

The irrigation system includes irrigation zones separated by exposure and solar orientation, master valves and flow sensors, and water-conserving full head-to-head coverage coupled with a satellite controller that monitors the weather and adjusts the amount of irrigation according to temperature, humidity, wind, rainfall, and other conditions.

Overall, the center saves approximately 215,000 gallons of water annually, compared to a similar building with conventional systems.

Green building materials

Low-VOC paints were used throughout the science and technology center. Many building materials had significant recycled content, including the acoustical ceiling tiles, Trex® synthetic wood benches, the toilet partitions, and even the structural steel. The acoustical ceiling tiles, for example, have between 61 and 78 percent pre-consumer recycled content.

Very little carpet was used in the center, to create flexibility for program changes and expansion within the building, as well as to meet the specific program requirements of the science labs. Any installed carpet met the criteria of the Carpet and Rug Institute's (CRI's) Indoor Air Quality Carpet "Green Label" protocol. The carpet is also 100 percent recyclable.

All of the new furniture is Greenguard Certified.

Beverly Hills High School Science and Technology Center

PEOPLE,
THAT TWO
BIRTHDAY.

THE HUBBLE TELESCOPE
WEIGHS 12 TONS, IS 43 FEET
LONG, AND COST $2.1
BILLION TO ORIGINALLY
BUILD.

OF FUEL REMAINED WHEN
LE LANDED ON THE MOON.

galileo

$F = MA$

physics

Landscape architecture

The most prominent landscape architecture element is, of course, the courtyard and its central oak tree, which provides both shade and a tangible connection to California's (natural) history. A bench ringing the oak tree invites students to sit, enjoy nature, and interact.

A majority of the courtyard is landscaped with bamboo, which is one of the fastest-growing plant species on earth and, therefore, contributes to carbon dioxide reduction. Bamboo also provides a green screen to shield some building façades from direct sunlight, while contributing to the site's beauty.

Outcome

Beverly Hills High School has always been a landmark in one of America's best-known communities. With the completion of the science and technology center, the high school not only has a new up-to-date facility, it provides the community with a 21st-century "green landmark"—a building that consumes 24 percent less energy and 24 percent less water than a comparable building, and serves as a living laboratory for green buildings and technologies.

Beverly Hills High School Science and Technology Center

CHAPTER 7

Hector Godinez Fundamental High School

**Santa Ana, California
2006**

The City of Santa Ana in Orange County, California had a problem: a congested urban environment, too few community recreation facilities, and too little open space.

The Santa Ana Unified School District also had a problem. It had too many high school students, not enough high schools, and not enough land on which to construct a new school.

The district only had a 5.5-acre site. Most new high schools are constructed on 40 to 45 acres.

But this site was adjacent to an undeveloped 20.5-acre section of the City of Santa Ana's Centennial Regional Park. That section, in turn, was near the Rancho Santiago Community College to the north. To the south of the park was the Discovery Museum of Orange County.

So, the district partnered with the City of Santa Ana, the Community College, and the Museum, each of which donated land for a new high school. But not enough land, at least at first glance.

The Santa Ana USD had assembled a 25.67-acre site for the Hector Godinez Fundamental High School which would have 2,500 students and stress a college prep curriculum, along with performing arts and athletics.

It was up to LPA, Inc., in collaboration with the Santa Ana USD, the City of Santa Ana, the College, and the Museum, to make the site work for the community.

"The site for our new high school required a truly unique solution to satisfy the needs of a diverse group of organizations contributing land for its development," says Jerry Hills, Manager of Construction, Santa Ana Unified School District. "A collaborative process was required to bring these groups together and develop consensus."

That collaboration created a $65.5-million sustainable "civic center" with a Main Street, green buildings, and joint-use facilities. Funding for Hector Godinez Fundamental High School—which had no land acquisition costs—was provided by both the State of California State School Bond and a local school bond passed by the Santa Ana Unified School District.

Planning began in June 2003. LPA, Inc. served as master planner, architect, and landscape architect on this project. Construction was completed in June 2006, with the school opening to its first students in September 2006.

Joint-use campus

The four project partners share the use of a three-story parking structure with 514 spaces, as well as a 450-seat performing arts complex that includes a workshop and a black-box theater, a gymnasium, hard courts, playing fields for soccer, football, and track and field, a nature center, and even classrooms. The joint-use facilities are located adjacent to the Centennial Regional Park, which supports off-hour community use of these amenities.

Proximity to the adjacent community college and museum supports joint-use science programs, cross-age tutoring, and adult education programs.

In addition, the campus hub, a "Main Street" (see below) provides a new civic space for both students and Santa Ana residents.

These joint-use facilities significantly reduced the amount of land the high school needed, which helped the campus fit onto the 25.67-acre site.

Compact development

The project team also met the space requirements for the 260,000-square-foot high school by creating a compact development site plan. LPA, Inc. began by giving the buildings a north–south orientation, which supported a more compact campus design.

The heart of the high school campus—the organizational hub—is the "Main Street," a traditional gathering place that stretches east–west across the site. As in any traditional small town, Main Street is the social center of the campus.

Lining the north side of Main Street are the joint-use gymnasium and the performing arts complex. Playing fields are located to the north and east of the gymnasium. Further north is Rancho Santiago Community College. To the east of the gymnasium and performing arts complex is Centennial Regional Park, which has, among other amenities, a lake.

Lining the south side of Main Street are the one-story administration and music buildings, a two-story media center building which has student classrooms, technology student services, a staff lounge on the ground floor, and the library on the second floor. The cafeteria and staff offices front Main Street and the classroom wing (see below).

The street was given a true Main Street design, including landscaping and street furniture, traditional concrete pavers, banners, and varied building materials, colors, and designs that physically link the high school to the surrounding community.

Extending south from the western end of Main Street is a long two-story classroom wing, with a three-story parking structure at the northwestern side of the wing. Further to the south is the Discovery Museum of Orange County.

Extending south from the administration building is the music building. The administration and music buildings on the east and the classroom wing on the west create a buffered zone in the heart of the campus for a student courtyard and the "science village"—two curvilinear clusters of science classrooms and labs.

To the east and southeast of the science village is a 7.0-acre nature center, an open space preserve with three mounds that showcase California native plant communities, including coastal chaparral, sage scrub, and riparian species, as well as a small wetlands.

This compact campus design enables students to quickly and easily walk to any building. It also separates the educational center of the campus from the major joint-use facilities, which creates a greater sense of academic community.

Architectural design

The classroom wing was designed as flexible "villages," enabling the classrooms to be grouped by subject discipline, grade level, or in interdisciplinary clusters.

The two science village buildings have green screen walls and berms, which connect them both visually and through their building materials to the adjacent nature center and wetlands.

LPA, Inc. scaled all of the buildings according to their context and to provide connections and transitions between different uses and spaces both on and adjacent to the high school campus. The urban character of the Main Street, for example, was supported by two-story buildings and large-scale "civic" buildings like the performing arts center and gymnasium, which created a visual transition between downtown Santa Ana, a neighboring industrial park, and the high school.

The two-story classroom wing provides a visual and noise buffer to the industrial park to the west of the campus. The single-story music building and science village help to create visual connections to the single-story Discovery Heritage Museum.

Open space and landscaping are used throughout the campus to connect the high school to the Centennial Regional Park.

Green features

This unique joint-use high school is also green.

It was constructed on the site of a former school that had modular buildings and had become an eyesore in the area. Reusing this site preserved open space elsewhere in the Santa Ana community.

The compact development also helped to preserve open space. The one-story science village buildings, for example, were placed adjacent to the nature center so that no grading or earthwork would encroach on this protected zone.

The campus buildings were also oriented to make maximum use of natural daylight and natural ventilation.

Landscaping and heat island mitigation

The landscape plan was designed to reinforce a sense of place, to honor the pre-existing land forms, to support circulation, to beautify the campus, and to mitigate heat islands.

Native oak and sycamore trees as well as other drought-tolerant canopy trees were used throughout the campus—between buildings, in courtyards, and along Main Street—to provide heat island mitigation. Main Street is lined with southern live oaks, which extend into the east and west courtyards. The remaining courtyards, which include the entry plaza and hard courts, are defined by a grid of Tipuana tipus and Koelreuterias, which are faster growing species and will quickly provide shade for the hardscape and seating areas.

Earth berms and green screens were placed along the walls to insulate the science village buildings from heat gain, reducing their HVAC use and energy consumption. These features also provide a green transition into the nature center.

The science village mounds are landscaped with cultivars of California natives, including coastal chaparral varieties of baccharis, rhus interguifolla, coast live oak, and California sycamore. The wetland areas have grass species of California sedge and rush varieties, which are accustomed to both perennial wet and dry conditions. Western poplars and willow trees, which are found in local riparian conditions, also beautify the campus.

Planning and architectural choices also provided heat island mitigation.

The parking structure provides 80 percent of the joint-use campus' parking needs, which prevents heat islands. Rather than surface parking lots—which are massive heat islands—providing 100 percent of the campus parking, they provide only 20 percent of the parking. This choice also preserved open space, which further mitigates heat islands and provides stormwater management (open space absorbs rain).

In addition, the classroom wing presents a reflecting wall to the nature center and acts as a sunscreen for the facility.

Natural daylighting and outdoor views

The buildings were oriented and designed to maximize natural daylighting. All windows have Low-E glazing to let in light and keep out solar heat. In general, the western walls have few windows and doors, to prevent heat migrating into the building interiors. Southern and eastern walls have glazed windows and sunshades to allow in light without heat.

The east–west facing classroom wing has floor-to-ceiling windows on the eastern façade, extensive light wells in the central corridors, and skylights on the second floor to bring natural lighting into the classrooms and hallways, reducing the use (and energy consumption) of artificial light.

Clerestories bring ample natural daylighting into the gymnasium. South-facing clerestories are shaded by metal fins that direct light into the building while keeping out solar heat.

South- and west-facing windows on all of the buildings are shaded with a variety of design elements, including roof overhangs, floor overhangs (on two-story buildings), Kalwall canopies, and extended aluminum mullions to help prevent interior solar heat gain while letting in light.

Artificial lighting system

Energy-efficient direct and indirect lighting systems with T8 lamps and individual controls have automatic occupancy sensors, which turn off lights in unoccupied spaces, further reducing energy use.

HVAC

The majority of buildings have high-efficiency rooftop packaged HVAC units. The performing arts complex, however, has an air-cooled chiller system and an energy-efficient underfloor air displacement system. None of the HVAC systems use CFC-based refrigerants.

The final HVAC choice was the dominant building material used on the campus: shot-blasted concrete blocks. As walls, they provide thermal massing—they absorb heat during the day, rather than letting heat transfer directly into rooms, and they release the heat slowly at night. Thermal massing lowers each building's cooling requirements in warm months, and during the winter it provides the insulation that helps to keep the building interiors warm, which lowers each building's heating requirements.

Water conservation and stormwater management

LPA, Inc. specified water-conserving plumbing fixtures to meet state-mandated requirements. The irrigation system uses low evapotranspiration rotors, sprays, and bubblers to provide appropriate water levels with minimal overspray and evaporation. The computer-based system, which has flow and rain sensors, adjusts irrigation according to the campus's microclimates, local weather conditions, solar exposure, and other criteria to deliver the right amount of water at the right time.

Stormwater from building roofs and runoff from adjacent paved areas is piped to the nature center's wetlands, where it is polished and allowed to regenerate ground water. Where land grades, uses, or available sites prohibited draining to a bioswale system, filters or other devices were used to treat the water prior to discharge into the storm drain system. All other hardscape areas drain to planters throughout the campus to limit drains and catch basins in paved areas and provide water polishing where possible.

Green building materials

Low- and zero-VOC paints, sealants, and adhesives were used throughout the campus. Materials with significant recycled content include plastic composite wall siding, which provides additional heat mitigation in the administration and music buildings and the science village.

No chalkboards or carpeting were installed in the classrooms, promoting a healthier indoor environment. Instead, the classrooms have white boards and vinyl composition tile flooring.

Outcome

Hector Godinez Fundamental High School's energy performance is 10 percent better than California's Title 24 requirements, the strictest energy code in the nation.

The school's water consumption is 30 percent less than a comparable conventional high school.

Hector Godinez Fundamental High School is a sought-after campus because of its outstanding facilities and its high academic standards. "This high school successfully addresses the needs of the community in every aspect of its use," say LPA, Inc.'s Rick D'Amato. "The design relates metaphorically to Santa Ana's cultural and historical identity, it provides architectural diversity through its use of form, scale, and materials, and it successfully educates through its programs and sustainability."

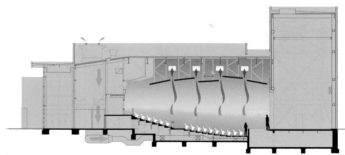

Displacement ventilation.

Hector Godinez Fundamental High School

Hector Godinez Fundamental High School

CHAPTER **8**

Marco Antonio Firebaugh High School

**Lynwood, California
2005**

Marco Antonio Firebaugh High School—named for a former member of the California Assembly—opened in Lynwood, California in September 2005. Firebaugh is much more than a high school serving 1,600 students. It is a multi-use education and community facility that has a community meeting space, a library, performing arts Center, gymnasium, athletic fields, and park space.

And it is green.

This school originated in 2000 when the Lynwood Unified School District (LUSD) faced a dilemma. Over the past decade, the population of school age children in the district had unexpectedly and rapidly grown from 14,000 students in 1990 to 20,000 students in 2000. The district had instituted temporary relief measures, primarily trailers for classrooms on former playgrounds and playing fields, but it knew much more needed to be done. In 2000, the LUSD created a Facilities Master Plan to build four new schools to serve 20,000 students. Marco Antonio Firebaugh High School was one of those schools.

In 2002, the LUSD hired LPA, Inc. to prepare the Marco Antonio Firebaugh High School site plan and provide architecture, interior design, and landscape architecture design.

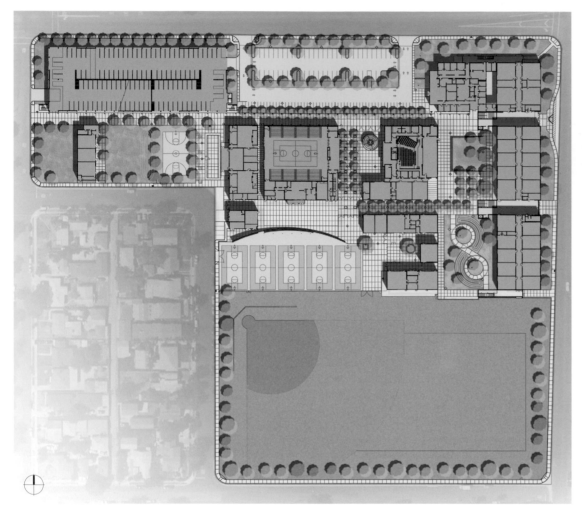

Displacement ventilation.

Marco Antonio Firebaugh High School

Construction began in March 2004. The classrooms were completed in September 2005 in time for the school's scheduled opening. The remaining campus facilities were completed in October 2005.

The $39.5-million budget was funded entirely by the State.

Joint-use campus

The LUSD faced several other dilemmas, including a shortage of land on which to construct Marco Antonio Firebaugh High School, the imperative to protect Lynwood's few remaining parks, and a need for more community facilities.

Working with the city and the LUSD, LPA, Inc.'s site plan addressed all of these challenges. The city created a 14.42-acre site for the school adjacent to the existing John Ham Park, one block west of I-710 and north of the I-105 freeway, in a densely developed area with residential neighborhoods on three sides of the site, and industrial development on the east side of the site adjacent to the freeway.

LPA, Inc. preserved the park and used it to provide part of the school's athletic and recreational facilities, turning it into a joint-use amenity. To squeeze the most uses out of the constrained school site, LPA, Inc. planned one- and two-story structures, building up rather than out to create a compact campus.

LPA, Inc. planned six buildings: a three-level parking structure with 360 parking spaces; a two-story building for administration offices, the library, and classrooms; two one-story classroom buildings; a one-story gymnasium; and a one-story, 40-foot-tall, 280-seat performing arts center. The parking structure, library, performing arts center, and gymnasium are joint-use facilities shared with the Lynwood community.

LPA, Inc. designed the campus as a series of distinct "academic cores": an arts core, physical education core, a science core, and a humanities core. Within the humanities core are four villages programmed to provide maximum flexibility. Each village has its own computer labs, teacher work areas, and conference rooms. The flexible villages can be organized by discipline (mathematics, English, social science, language), by interdisciplinary instruction, by educational academies, or by grade level.

To make the high school a good neighbor, LPA, Inc. sited the buildings fronting major thoroughfares to emphasize their importance to the community and located athletic fields adjacent to residences for shared use. Public use facilities—the library, performing arts center, gymnasium and parking structure—were placed along Martin Luther King Jr. Boulevard, a major arterial running along the northern end of the site, to promote easy public access while providing security for students and the academic facilities.

A student parking structure was sited on the northwest corner of the campus along Martin Luther King Jr. Boulevard and adjacent to a small, heavily landscaped surface parking lot for guest, faculty, and administration vehicles. These provide both a buffer for, and access to, the performing arts center and the gymnasium on the west end of the campus where it opens onto the hard surface courts and the park beyond.

The parking was located so that it provides direct access to the Boulevard of Achievement, a major 18-foot-wide tree-lined pedestrian circulation spine that parallels Martin Luther King Jr. Boulevard. The Boulevard of Achievement extends the length of the site running east to west, linking the joint-use facilities.

This walkway is lined with graphic art work detailing the achievements of successful people in various fields from the local community and beyond to provide inspiration to students on a daily basis as they enter the campus. The Boulevard was designed so that the names of graduating students who achieve success in their adult lives can be added in the future.

The major academic facilities were sited around a central quad and a grass amphitheater with a concrete stage that is used for school assemblies, pep rallies, and even as an outdoor classroom.

Another major outdoor facility is the school cafeteria: a 10,000-square-foot outdoor dining area protected by a translucent roofing system. Other outdoor spaces include courtyards and an arts patio.

The site plan then consolidated all of that development on the northern half of the property, devoting 75 percent of the site to open space, recreational, and athletic uses, and the park.

Architectural design

The architectural design incorporated grey sandblasted concrete blocks, white plaster, white steel columns and canopies, and green insulated glass into a modern architectural design.

Walls of glass and large cantilevered overhangs constructed with translucent roof panels define the building entries and pedestrian circulation routes. Bold accent colors—maroon, gold, and blue—strategically placed on interior walls complement the campus's neutral color palette. Students and administrators liked the accent colors so much that they adopted maroon and gold as the school's colors.

Green features

Perhaps the greatest challenge LPA, Inc. faced in its green design for Marco Antonio Firebaugh High School was the site plan and the building orientation necessitated by that site plan. LPA, Inc. had to site the joint-use facilities for easy community access from Martin Luther King Jr. Boulevard on the north end of the campus. That gave the two-story classroom building and other facilities a due west orientation, making solar exposure a significant problem that LPA, Inc. mitigated with design.

Heat island mitigation
Rather than massive surface parking lots, which are major heat islands, LPA, Inc. instead designed a three-story parking structure and created a small landscaped surface parking lot for faculty, administrators, and visitors.

Large overhangs on many buildings help minimize outside heat islands and interior solar heat gain. The translucent roof panels over pedestrian corridors and exterior stairways provide filtered sunlight without heat gain.

As always, landscape architecture was also used to provide significant heat island mitigation.

Landscape architecture
More than 75 percent of the 14.42-acre site is landscaped open space, including the playing fields, the quad, and amphitheater. Open space provides the best heat island mitigation.

Drought tolerant plants were used throughout the landscape plan.

Natural daylighting and outdoor views

Large windows and sidelights along entry doors bring natural daylight and outdoor views to 100 percent of the academic spaces. The lobby of the administration building has a two-story glass wall.

Indoor spaces used for art classes have large overhead rolling doors that bring natural ventilation and daylight into those classrooms. The gymnasium has 10 five-foot-square skylights that provide enough natural daylighting so that the artificial lighting system is not needed during the day.

The cafeteria's translucent roof system provides filtered natural light, ventilation, and outdoor views.

HVAC

The school's mechanical HVAC systems are zoned according to each space's solar orientation, thereby reducing unnecessary energy use while maintaining comfort for students and staff. All of the academic spaces have operable windows and overhead rolling doors, which can provide natural ventilation.

For the administration building, LPA, Inc. designed the two-story glass lobby to act as a giant heat stack. In-floor linear diffusers and low-velocity displacement ventilation along the face of the glass allows hot air to rise to air grilles hidden above the lobby's perforated metal ceiling, where the air is vented back to HVAC equipment. The lobby also acts as a buffer that reduces heat gain in the second-floor library, reducing direct heat gain from the western exposure.

To further reduce HVAC usage, LPA, Inc. placed the circulation stairs on the outside of buildings, which also helps to lower noise levels in those facilities.

Outcome

Marco Antonio Firebaugh High School is a success by many measures.

By virtue of its green design, this high school consumes less energy and water than a comparable conventional high school, and therefore, its overall operating costs are lower than comparable non-green schools.

Because of the extensive natural light and fresh air in the buildings, the high school offers a healthier and more productive learning environment for students and better working conditions for teachers and staff.

Because of this campus's many joint uses—educational, athletic, performing arts, and parkland—this high school is a prominent and much-used landmark for its community.

Marco Antonio Firebaugh High School

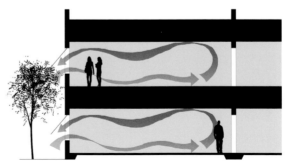

Natural ventilation.

CHAPTER 9

Environmental Nature Center

Newport Beach, California
2008

The single-story, 9,000-square-foot Environmental Nature Center (ENC) in Newport Beach, California earned a LEED-Platinum rating when it was completed in 2008. LPA, Inc. provided programming, planning, architecture, interior design, and landscape architecture services on this project.

The $4.7-million Environmental Nature Center is a net zero energy/carbon building and the first LEED-Platinum building in Orange County.

The ENC was constructed on just under one acre to preserve as much of the existing 3.5-acre site and its demonstration gardens and habitats as possible. The site is adjacent to Newport Harbor High School.

Project goals

The Environmental Nature Center, a nonprofit public benefit corporation, had several goals for this new facility:

- To serve as a living laboratory and educational tool for smart green building design.
- To create a campus with the necessary facilities to meet its educational mission.
- To provide educational programs that create lasting impressions on the lives of visitors, and to provide life-changing opportunities for visitors to experience and learn about their relationship with nature.
- To attract, develop, nurture, and retain the most talented staff, board, and volunteers.

To meet these goals, LPA, Inc. created a multipurpose building that holds a museum, creative studio classroom, laboratory, a combination library and conference room, a nature store, a deck that serves as an amphitheater terrace, staff and work areas, a combination kitchen and volunteer room, a copy and equipment room, storage rooms, and restrooms.

Architectural design

The design integrates the Environmental Nature Center into its natural surroundings, particularly the temperate Newport Beach climate, through a building placement that takes advantage of the prevailing coastal breezes. The building's natural materials and the use of earth-tone colors visually connect the facility to its coastal setting. The shape of the building, moreover, not only promotes natural ventilation, it also creates the most efficient angle for the use of photovoltaic panels.

The terrace surrounding the existing Butterfly House is an extension of the teaching area—the campfire pit and the small amphitheater are used as an outdoor classroom—and it is an entrance to the 14 native gardens on the ENC grounds.

LPA, Inc.'s design theme for the building interior was "less is more." Thus, rather than installing tile or carpeting or linoleum in the classrooms and museum, the concrete slab was polished and serves as the floor. Similarly, as part of the natural ventilation systems in the classrooms, LPA, Inc. had the contractor simply expose the wall framing and not install any drywall above 15 feet. This "opening" in the wall vents the classroom spaces and allows the warm air in the space to exit the building through the operable windows in the north wall.

Green features

To earn the LEED-Platinum rating for the Environmental Nature Center, LPA, Inc. employed a wide variety of planning and design strategies and technologies that are applicable to any kind of building. An LPA, Inc.-designed comprehensive signage program educates visitors and staff about the smart green design used throughout the Center.

Heat island mitigation

LPA, Inc. used light-colored concrete, rather than heat-absorbing asphalt, for parking, walkways, and other paved areas.

The standing seam metal roof has been coated with a color that meets the Solar Reflectance Index of 0.29 for heat sink reduction by LEED standards.

Landscape architecture provides further heat island mitigation by shading building walls and paved areas. The landscaping, including that in the parking lot and the surrounding ecosystems of the Nature Center, also creates an evaporative cooling effect, further reducing heat islands and air conditioning requirements.

Natural daylighting

A north–south building orientation brings abundant natural daylight into the Environmental Nature Center. The Low-E glass eliminates the need for any shading devices. The operable windows at the lowest and highest points vent the building and allow the occupants to "tune" the interior temperature based on climate conditions.

Artificial lighting system

The artificial lighting system uses energy-efficient direct and indirect lighting with T-8 lamps, dimming systems, and occupancy sensors to reduce the system's energy consumption.

Natural HVAC

The building's north–south orientation takes advantage of the prevailing ocean breezes to naturally ventilate all interior spaces, which eliminates the need for air conditioning. Operable windows and the sloped roof over the classroom and exhibit space draw cooling ocean breezes in, through, and out of the building.

The building doesn't even have an artificial heating system. Passively, the space takes advantage of the low sun entering the space in the winter months, which heats the exposed concrete floor slab. Heat then rises from the floor, warming the building interior.

Energy conservation and generation

Eliminating the need for a conventional HVAC system, filling the interior with natural daylight, and other strategies discussed above all provide significant energy conservation.

The ENC also has south-facing rooftop photovoltaic panels, which generate 95 percent of the Center's electricity requirements. A demonstration wind turbine provides additional electrical power.

Water conservation and stormwater management

Waterless urinals and dual flush and low-flow toilet fixtures save an average of 15,000 gallons of potable water annually. The drought-tolerant and indigenous plant materials of the landscape architecture eliminate the need for an irrigation system, further saving water.

The ENC takes advantage of natural rainfall. Water is collected from the roof of the administration building and directed into a large decorative pot below, which then drains to perforated piping in a nearby vegetated area, concentrating the water where it is needed. Water also falls from runnels on the roof of the main building into a drainage basin, and is then directed to a planted area.

Stormwater flows across the parking lot to a detention basin filled with native California plants. The stormwater is partially filtered by these plants as it is absorbed into the ground, eliminating runoff. Because no irrigation system was installed on site, the stormwater is also useful to water the plants in this area.

Green building materials

LPA, Inc.'s green building materials choices went a long way toward making the Environmental Nature Center more sustainable.

Color was integrated into the exterior plaster, so no painting was required, which reduced the project cost, conserved natural resources, and reduced the project's VOC emissions. It also saves money over the long-term, because the façade won't have to be repainted every few years.

The ENC's primary exterior siding is composed of recycled wood and plastic scraps that would normally end up in a landfill. The siding is colorfast, and it requires virtually no upkeep.

The building insulation is made of 85 percent recycled denim material and 15 percent cotton fibers, a rapidly renewable resource. A portion of the interior wall has been exposed with a transparent material to demonstrate and showcase this recycled and renewable resource.

The countertops, which are fully recyclable, are made of natural linoleum that is composed of 100 percent organic materials, including linseed oil,

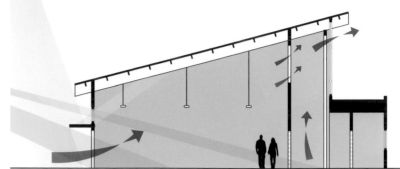
Natural ventilation.

resins, wood flour, and a natural jute backing. Pressed biofiber wheatboard, which was used for millwork and shelving units, offers a rich golden alternative to traditional hardwood or panel products. The wheat straw and sunflower hulls, which were used for the wheatboard, are recovered waste from pre-consumer agricultural production.

The carpet tiles in the office and library wing of the facility have a high recycled content and meet the Carpet Green label for post-industrial reuse. Recycled fabrics were used in the furnishings and workstations.

Eighty-two percent of the construction waste was diverted from landfills and recycled.

Outcome

The LEED-Platinum Environmental Nature Center exceeds California's Title 24 requirements, the strictest in the nation, by 70 percent for the exterior and 63 percent for the interior. The facility basically creates all of the power that it consumes.

The ENC uses 46 percent less water than a comparable conventional building. The Center is projected to save $20,000 annually in operating costs.

Of particular importance, the Environmental Nature Center is a net zero energy/net carbon building. It uses energy-efficient design and technologies—and renewable energy technologies, not fossil fuels— to generate all of its power requirements.

The ENC, which has served Orange County for more than 25 years, now has a facility that can generate positive change in the community on a daily basis with its many different programs for the general public and its K–7 students.

Environmental Nature Center

CHAPTER 10

Green Modernizations and Expansions of Existing Schools

The greenest thing a school district can do is to make its existing schools more sustainable.

Green modernizations are even more sustainable than constructing new green schools.

"Reduce, Reuse, Recycle" is the mantra of the environmental movement, and it applies directly to the green modernization and expansion of an existing school.

A school district reduces its development footprint, because it is modernizing existing buildings or expanding on an already developed property, rather than using a greenfield site. The district reduces the amount of natural resources that it consumes by greening an existing school, because it doesn't have to construct a new building foundation, façade, or, for the most part, interior rooms. Thus, the district also reduces the energy that it would have consumed and the greenhouse gases that it would have generated if had purchased the building materials for those components from distant suppliers.

Green modernization and expansion projects also reduce the amount of money that a school district spends. New construction costs much more than modernization and expansion.

With a green modernization, the district reuses existing school facilities in new and sustainable ways. Often, it also reuses some of the school's existing furnishings.

Finally, a green modernization and/or expansion project generates less waste than new construction, and it can recycle its demolition and construction waste, often into new uses on site.

On top of all of these benefits, green modernization and expansion projects bring all of the benefits of new green school construction to students, teachers, administrators, staff, the school district, the larger community … and they do more.

A green modernization generates greater school pride in students, faculty, and staff. It also reinvigorates the community, often leading to the rehabilitation of properties in surrounding residential neighborhoods.

Like new construction, green modernization and expansion projects also generate significant savings in long-term operating costs, strengthen faculty and staff attraction and retention rates, and improve student learning and test scores.

Clearly, green modernization and expansion projects are a tremendous opportunity for school districts to meet the growing number of municipal and state regulations about green buildings, improve their overall sustainability, reduce their greenhouse gas footprint, improve their relationship with the larger community, and better serve their students, faculty, administrators, and staff—all at a lower cost than new construction projects would entail.

Green modernization process

As with new construction, a green modernization and expansion project is a comprehensive strategy that requires a collaborative planning, design, and construction process in which all project team members work together from the start of the project, managing upfront the interplay and integration of each green component with the rest of the project.

The first step in the green modernization process, therefore, is to assemble a green project team, from architect and landscape architect to engineers, contractors, and outside consultants, as well as school district and school administrators and staff.

Site design committee

Next, establish a site design committee that will work with the project team to create a "wish list" of things that need to be improved on the existing school campus, particularly those features that cause compromises in—or even impair—the educational program. Many schools that are more than 25 years old, for example, have inflexible self-contained classrooms that don't support new teaching and learning modalities or clustering.

In addition, these schools usually don't have enough space to support staff collaboration, counseling, psychologist, speech, resource specialist programs, or parent-teacher work.

Finally, the site design committee and the project team should discuss classroom and other interior components that should go on the wish list, from teaching walls to technology access.

School survey

The project team then surveys and photographs the entire school. LPA, Inc., for example, uses its patented "Accu-Survey" process that verifies existing conditions, examines every building system, and identifies what can be improved.

The school survey will include interviews with the school's and the district's maintenance staff to identify key long-term issues, from the need for painting or a new roof to HVAC, plumbing, and lighting upgrades.

The project team and the maintenance staff also assemble existing documents showing the original construction details and any changes or upgrades that have been made since the school was first built.

Schematic design

Based on the information gathered from the site design committee and the school survey, the project team then creates a schematic design that establishes the general scope, defines the conceptual design, establishes the scale, and identifies the relationship of each project component to every other component in the overall modernization project and to the rest of the school. The schematic design, for example, shows how a landscaping feature will impact HVAC requirements.

Models and drawings are created to give the school district and school administrators a visual understanding of the project. This is the foundation on which the design development process will go forward.

Set your budget

At the same time, the project team works with the district and school administrators to develop a project budget that establishes the approximate cost for each planned component in the green modernization plan. Incorporated into the project budget are the grants, rebates, and other financial aids and incentives available for this project. The project budget should also be based upon, and incorporate, the following:

- An estimated first costs analysis.
- A life cycle analysis.
- A pre-construction analysis that will include issues such as the impact of a new lighting system or an Energy Star roof on HVAC requirements and usage.
- An environmental value analysis. How well does each green component benefit the environment? Does it reduce energy, conserve water, lower greenhouse gas emissions, or improve the indoor air quality?
- An estimated ROI analysis.
- A LEED/CHPS analysis to determine which components will earn the most credits if the school district wants the project to earn a LEED or CHPS rating.

Remember: Making a larger upfront investment, like installing an entirely new artificial lighting system instead of just switching to energy-conserving lamps, often provides greater long-term financial and environmental benefits.

Together, the schematic design and the project budget will define the parameters of this particular green modernization project and create reasonable expectations for the school district and school administrators. This package is submitted to the district design committee for approval.

Design development

In this phase, the project team finalizes all of the details of the green modernization project's design and construction, from the scale and dimensions to the selection of specific building materials and more detailed decisions like locations of the electrical outlets.

In design development, long-term maintenance and operating issues and costs are also examined and incorporated into the overall design and material and technology choices.

The project team assesses the municipality's regulatory requirements and incorporates those requirements into the project design. The project team also reviews the district's standards specifications to assure that the modernization project complies with the school district's guidelines.

District review and comment

A set of drawings and design specifications—along with a second project cost estimate to demonstrate that the green modernization project complies with the established budget—is submitted to the school district for review and comment.

Based on the school district's review, the project team finalizes the project design, phasing, and construction plans.

Construction documents and bid process

The project team creates a complete, concise set of construction plans and specifications based upon the green modernization project's educational specifications and design development package. This construction bid package should create a structure for the construction process that generates few, if any, change orders during actual construction.

Construction

As with any green construction process, at least 50 percent of the green modernization project's demolition and construction waste should be recycled.

An Indoor Air Quality (IAQ) construction management plan should protect building interiors from construction dust and pollutants, both during construction and when the buildings are first used.

Green post-occupancy strategies

Once the green modernization project is completed, implement green maintenance and cleaning programs that don't use toxic materials and products.

Start comprehensive in-house recycling and waste reduction programs.

Measure the immediate results of implementing the green modernization plan against the original project goals.

Then, conduct a yearly commissioning to make sure that all green elements/systems are performing properly. In particular, measure the project's energy consumption and greenhouse gas emissions to make sure they meet regulatory requirements and the school district's green modernization goals.

Green modernization strategies

A green modernization can make significant improvements that bring many benefits to the school campus.

Replacing the existing landscaping with drought-tolerant mostly native plants, for example, greatly reduces water consumption and costs, as well as maintenance time and costs. Installing a water-conserving irrigation system—particularly one that uses greywater recycled from on-site uses—will also help lower water consumption and costs.

Replacing asphalt parking, roadway, and sidewalk surfaces with permeable paving supports both stormwater management and groundwater recharge. Bioswales in parking lots and around the building(s) help to both cleanse and reduce stormwater runoff, while beautifying the campus. Such landscape measures also reduce stormwater mitigation costs.

Shading west- and south-facing façades with green screens (metal lattices planted with vines or climbing flowers), replacing a dark standard roof with an Energy Star "cool roof" or green (landscaped) roof, and shading courtyards, walkways, and parking lots will greatly minimize the number and impact of a school's heat islands.

As for the building façade, replace inefficient glass with high-performance glazed windows that let in natural daylight while keeping out solar heat. Add external sunshades to prevent interior heat build-up and glare. Install an arcade or overhangs around low-rise buildings to provide heat island mitigation. Add insulation to existing wall cavities to increase the energy efficiency of the building envelope.

Studies by Carnegie Mellon University, the Heschong Mahone Group, and others have documented that outdoor views, natural daylight, and fresh air have a very positive impact on student learning and test scores, as well as on faculty job satisfaction, attraction, and retention.

So, any school's green modernization project should emphasize those features. How?

Install larger windows, clerestories, skylights, light monitors, light shelves, and/or atriums to bring natural daylight to the interior.

Many schools have energy-efficient HVAC systems, but those systems are often improperly programmed or configured, greatly lessening their energy efficiency. So, re-commission the school's HVAC system and install monitoring equipment to help assure that it continues to perform at optimal levels.

Replace inefficient HVAC systems with energy-efficient equipment that doesn't use ozone-depleting hydrochlorofluorocarbon (HCFC), Halon, or chlorofluorocarbon (CFC)-based refrigerants.

The HVAC system should also bring more filtered fresh air to the building interior. Install motion sensors that automatically turn off HVAC functions in unoccupied rooms to save energy.

To conserve traditional energy sources, and avoid burning fossil fuels that emit greenhouse gases, school districts can purchase renewable energy credits, so that they use wind power, biomass, geothermal, and/or small hydroelectric plants to power their schools.

The 10-Step Green
Modernization
Process

1. Assemble a green team

2. Site design committee—
    wish list

3. School survey

4. Schematic design

5. Set your budget

6. Design development—
    regulatory assessment,
    school district standards

7. School district review
    and comment

8. Construction documents
    and bid process

9. Green modernization
    construction

10. Green post-occupancy
    strategies

A green modernization project can also install its own renewable energy systems, like solar power. Renewable energy systems can often serve multiple uses. Photovoltaic panels have been used as canopies that shade walkways and parking lots. Renewable energy systems, such as wind turbines, can also be used as teaching tools for science and math classes.

Install water-conserving plumbing in kitchen facilities, restrooms, and gymnasium locker rooms, from automatic sensors on faucets to waterless urinals. Consider installing a greywater or black water recycling system that will provide water for toilet flushing and for landscaping irrigation.

Throughout the green modernization, use healthier green building materials, particularly low- and zero-VOC paints, sealants, glues, finishes, and furnishings, which will help improve the indoor air quality. Choose natural, rapidly renewable building materials, such as natural linoleum and bamboo flooring. Select building materials like carpeting, ceiling tiles, and furnishing with significant recycled content. All of these products are now readily available, and they typically cost no more than conventional often-toxic building materials.

CHAPTER 11

Green Modernization and Expansion School Projects

Three southern California high school districts implemented green modernization and expansion projects at four different schools that made those schools more functional, efficient, and attractive for students, faculty, administrators, and staff. These projects also improved the schools' overall sustainability, reduced their greenhouse gas footprint, and improved their relationships with their communities, all at a lower cost than new school construction projects would entail.

Lessons learned

The three schools showcased in this chapter exemplify the importance of three key lessons of green modernization and expansion school projects:

1. Hidden potential. Any school has existing facilities with tremendous potential to meet current and future needs, from under-utilized and overlooked structures to rooms and buildings that can serve entirely different uses. Incorporating these spaces into the green modernization and expansion master plan can limit the amount of new construction needed and also minimize the amount of reconstruction necessary within existing buildings, significantly reducing the project cost.

2. The power of reorganization. Simply reorganizing a school campus according to discipline by relocating education and athletic programs can create a more functional and cohesive school and minimize new construction requirements.

3. Multi-purpose landscape architecture. In addition to heat island mitigation, natural stormwater management, and campus beautification, landscape architecture can be used to "re-brand" a school, create view corridors, support wayfinding, move classes outside, and enhance social gatherings and interactions.

The following case studies put those three lessons into action in ways unique to each school.

Thurston Middle School

Thurston Middle School in Laguna Beach, California had never been modernized and the buildings were beginning to decline. The facilities had also not kept up with the changes and advances in the school's educational programs. Nor did the campus reflect the high-quality education the school provided or the values of the surrounding community.

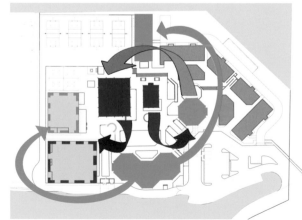

PROGRAM SHIFT
Administration Office moves to existing library

PROGRAM SHIFT
Relocate Library & Computer Lab to existing Multi-Purpose Room

PROGRAM SHIFT
Multi Purpose Room Function incorporated into New Gymnasium Program

PROGRAM SHIFT
Existing Technology, Science and Art Building expands number of teaching stations

A committee of city officials, school district administrators, Thurston Middle School administrators, civic organizations, and community clubs worked for several years to determine the school's physical and educational needs. Then, 80 percent of the voters approved a bond measure to fund a green modernization of Thurston Middle School.

LPA, Inc. provided integrated master planning, architecture, landscape architecture, interior design, and graphic design services on this project.

To meet the goals of the community, the school district, and the school administrators for the school, LPA, Inc. and the rest of the project team completely reconstructed the existing campus facilities and reorganized the programming spaces.

The team removed two portable/temporary buildings, creating room for new facilities on the campus without expanding the development footprint.

Four buildings were reprogrammed, which minimized the amount of new construction needed on the campus.

The original library building at the front of the campus became the new administration building, welcoming students, parents, and visitors to the school. It also has a staff lounge and patio.

The original administration building became three new classrooms: a biology classroom, a biology lab, and a technology/computer lab. The original multi-purpose room became the new library. An existing

abandoned locker shelter became a computer lab/technology classroom. A new art classroom and new drama and band/instrument rooms were added to existing buildings on the campus.

The project modernized the school's kitchen and the home economics classroom.

The project team constructed two new buildings: a 10,000-square-foot gymnasium with a locker room and seating for up to 500 people, as well as a black box performing arts center complex. Both the gymnasium and performing arts complex are joint-use facilities shared with the community.

The project team also transformed a former locker shelter that had been scheduled for demolition and turned it into a new wireless technology workshop. The column and roof structure were retained. Glass north, south, and east walls were added. The western wall is solid to help prevent interior solar heat gain. From inside the workshop, the walls, which are interspersed with white marker and tack boards, overlook landscaped patios and courtyards. By reusing the locker shelter, the project team created a valuable new classroom at a fraction of the cost of constructing an entirely new building and in far less time, and it minimized disruption to the rest of the campus.

Throughout the school, the project team improved the classroom environment by making the classrooms more spacious and user-friendly with features like substantial wall space to display student work and projects, and by giving the rooms daylighting and wiring them for different technology uses.

The project team's work extended far beyond the buildings to modernize the entire campus site. By evaluating the student circulation patterns and the layout of existing mature trees, the team created outdoor classrooms with concrete seat walls, shade, planters, and berms and natural seating areas made by reusing soil from the grading and construction work on the campus. These outdoor classrooms reduced the amount of impermeable surfaces on the campus (which supports stormwater management), saved the healthy mature trees, and added new plantings.

A new translucent canopy entry to the gymnasium and drama room, for example, serves as an outdoor classroom for drama student rehearsals.

In addition to the new gymnasium, the athletics department got new outdoor hard courts, expanded and enhanced athletic fields, and a new and rigorous obstacle course.

New native and drought-tolerant landscaping throughout the campus provides visual and natural connections to the surrounding canyon, and it mitigates heat islands, reducing HVAC use in the buildings and energy consumption.

The project team renovated the central quad to provide strong, attractive, and identifiable entries to the administration building, the gymnasium, and the lunch shelter. This renovation streamlined student circulation, preserved the existing trees, added new planting and softscape areas, and provided more seating areas.

Finally, the project team reconfigured the existing parking lots and vehicular circulation to create a more efficient pick-up/drop-off area, make the parking more accessible, and improve pedestrian circulation and safety. Trees and landscaped areas were added to mitigate heat islands.

Throughout this green modernization and expansion project, LPA, Inc. repeated the school's color palette on the new buildings to help integrate them into the campus, used durable materials, particularly concrete block, and fenestrated the new buildings to mitigate interior solar heat gain.

Green features throughout the campus include new windows and skylights in all exterior-facing classrooms that bring natural light into the school without solar heat gain, reducing the use of artificial lighting and energy consumption. Skylights, for example, run the entire length of both the new library and the gymnasium.

The energy-efficient artificial lighting system has motion sensors that adjust lighting in the rooms according to sunlight and activity, further reducing energy consumption. Drought-tolerant and native landscaping combined with high-efficiency irrigation systems help conserve water.

This major green modernization and expansion project transformed the campus for just $9.545 million, or $175 per square foot.

The green modernization of Thurston Middle School won California's top CASH (Coalition for Adequate School Housing) "Jury Excellence Award" in 2005.

Following the green modernization, more than 100 new students who had been in private schools enrolled at Thurston Middle School. Teachers report that students are now more engaged in their classes because of the new amenities and improved physical environment.

Laguna Beach High School

This high school—the only high school in the Laguna Beach Unified School District—has 1,060 students. It is located in the heart of Laguna Beach, California, a community of 25,000 residents that actively preserves its special environment of Pacific Ocean beaches, hills, canyons, and surrounding park land. Established in 1934, the 13.5-acre high school now provides most of the recreational open space in the 9.7-square-mile city.

Like Thurston Middle School, Laguna Beach High School had never been modernized and the buildings were beginning to decline. Not only had the facilities not kept up with the changes and advances in the school's educational programs, the educational programs and departments were scattered all over the campus, creating inefficiencies and challenges for students, faculty, and staff.

A 30-person site design committee with faculty representatives from each department, school administrators, and school district administrators identified the major goals for this green modernization and expansion project: relocate educational programs and departments to maximize efficient use of the facilities and to support departmental collaboration, improve all of the academic areas, bring technology into all of the classrooms, extend the classrooms outdoors, encourage interdisciplinary work, create new classrooms, state-of-the-art science labs, a new technology center, a new dance studio, and new state-of-the-art athletic facilities, and integrate all of the new buildings into the existing campus.

LPA, Inc. provided integrated master planning, architecture, landscape architecture, interior design, and graphic design services on this project.

LPA, Inc. and the project team reorganized the campus by moving the educational programs to new locations to create greater efficiency and interdisciplinary collaboration. This reorganization minimized the amount of new construction needed to accommodate targeted high school programs and classes, which lowered project costs and preserved open space.

The project team modernized all of the existing buildings by wiring each space for technology use, from computers to LCD projectors. The HVAC and lighting systems were replaced with energy-efficient technologies. The windows and doors were also replaced.

The old shop building was transformed into an art studio for ceramics/sculpting classes; an art studio for photography, painting, drawing, and graphic design; a TV studio; and technology labs. New connections between the first and second floor, including an elevator, were added to improve accessibility. The façade was redesigned to reinforce the front door to the stadium and to showcase the school's technology to the community.

Two new buildings were constructed to provide four new classrooms and a dance studio with locker rooms.

Before

The athletics complex was completely modernized. The boys' gym and the girls' gym were given new wood floor systems, new HVAC and interior lighting systems, and new interior paint and finishes.

The existing sports fields were replaced with college-level synthetic turf soccer, football, and track facilities. The original natural turf baseball field was renovated and "flipped" to increase the size of play areas, extend the outfields, and improve the safety of players, public visitors using the track, and adjacent roadways. New dugouts and batting cages were added. The bleachers were updated.

The athletic complex's visitor grandstands were completely renovated and given a new elevator, an enlarged staircase with amphitheater-style seating, and a second-story observation deck. A new concession stand, ticket booth with trellis, and restroom facilities were added to the complex. The project team also used the new ticket booth to provide a secondary entry to the complex and to integrate the lower level of the stadium into the main campus.

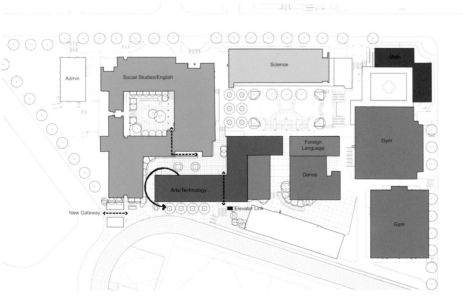

Pedestrian paths and circulation were significantly improved throughout the campus. Pathways, stairs, ramps, and walkways were redesigned to provide central access points that are easily identifiable from the adjacent streets. Overgrown pathways and pathways that led to building entrances no longer in use were removed. New accessible pathways were added and lined with pedestrian level lights and mid-level terraces for student and public seating.

Trees, including date palms, were placed to help identify the school entry and community plazas. Landscape architecture was also used to strengthen the school's integration into the Laguna Beach community by reinforcing the historic entry to the campus. The project team constructed a gently terraced lawn on which students can sit and socialize, enjoying views of the Pacific Ocean. Pathways to the stadium were transformed with outdoor seating and landscaping to create attractive and welcoming pre-function areas for community sports enthusiasts. These pathways also serve as outdoor classrooms for the adjacent art and technology classrooms.

Many of the existing outdoor areas on campus had fallen into disrepair, had minimal landscaping, and didn't provide adequate seating. This created a harsh environment, which meant that many of these spaces were unused. The project team removed the old cracked concrete, added large canopy trees such as California sycamores and coast live oak, used Douglas iris and other plants to create an attractive understory, provided integrated seating, and improved access to these areas.

LPA, Inc. also expanded and renovated an existing series of courtyards on the campus to create strong visual and physical linkages and to provide outdoor classrooms whose design and plantings relate directly to the educational programming of the adjacent classrooms.

LPA, Inc. renovated the senior quad, which had deteriorated over time, by giving it seat walls, shade trees, and other amenities. The primary central quad was also renovated and enhanced with a new fabric lunch shelter, which protects students from the sun and birds. The old dark red pavement was removed and replaced with a more neutral tan-colored paving. Sycamore trees were added around the lunch shelter to provide more shade and attractive areas for student gatherings and interactions.

The existing campus had been developed and expanded over six decades. It was left with a broad range of architectural styles. To bring greater physical unity to the campus, and to integrate the new buildings into the existing campus and the larger Laguna Beach community and environment, LPA, Inc. used landscape architecture and a neutral "tone on tone" color palette of ochre, green, and taupe on all of the new and

A new energy management system monitors the HVAC and lighting systems. The maintenance staff is able to track system energy use and identify and correct any inefficiencies.

Outside, drought-tolerant native landscaping shades southern, western, and eastern building exposures, pedestrian walkways, and seating areas, to mitigate heat islands. LPA, Inc. used native plants and the adopted plant palette of the local community to better integrate the campus into its neighborhood.

Significantly increasing the landscaped areas on the campus supports stormwater management. In addition, many landscape areas now drain into planters to provide irrigation, water clarification, and increase percolation. New landscaping in each of the campus courtyards now collects rainwater, controlling runoff from the hardscape and filtering the water before it enters the storm drain system. Much of the southern part of the campus was designed so that rainwater flows into the synthetic fields and natural turf baseball field where it is partially cleaned before entering the storm drains of the synthetic fields and before it percolates into aquifers under the natural turf field.

existing buildings. Outdoor classroom areas, for example, were painted with the colors of the surrounding natural environment—sandy beaches, canyons, riparian streams, and coastal hills.

Throughout Laguna Beach High School, the project team installed larger windows and used high-performance window glazing to bring abundant daylight into interior spaces while keeping out solar heat gain. The energy-efficient indirect lighting system has occupancy sensors which turn lights off when no one is in a room.

The green modernization and expansion of Laguna Beach High School—which renovated 121,500 square feet of existing space and constructed 10,000 square feet of new space—cost $17.5 million, or $115 per square foot.

Before

Westminster High School

Westminster High School in Westminster, California—which is also in the Huntington Beach Union High School District—was constructed in 1958, expanded in the early 1970s, and now serves 2,700 students. It used to be known as "the prison school."

Westminster High School had badly outdated buildings as well as poorly functioning air handling units, a clear window glazing that promoted significant interior solar heat gain, and even drapes from the late 1950s that were patched together with duct tape to cover the windows when necessary.

The Huntington Beach Union High School District wanted to upgrade and improve the learning environments and install energy efficient lighting, HVAC, and other technology systems.

LPA, Inc. served as master planner, architect, and landscape architect for this $40.5-million green modernization and expansion project, which received funding from Proposition 47 Energy Grants and rebates from the Savings By Design program for the installation of Solatubes in the classrooms, energy efficient window glazing, an energy-efficient HVAC system, and a cool roof.

Green Modernization and Expansion School Projects

Before

The school's existing courtyards were restored and given individual identities through landscaping, upgraded paving, concrete seating, graphics, signage, and color to serve as the main wayfinding strategy on the campus. In addition, the courtyards were redesigned with large shade trees, grass berms, and seat walls to serve as exterior extensions of adjacent classrooms. To preserve the existing fully mature trees in the courtyards, the project team modified the grading layout for the paving, removed existing hardscape, and increased the planting areas around the trees to promote water infiltration and deeper rooting.

An earlier seismic upgrade to the buildings provided an opportunity for the project team to create Orsogril green screens in the courtyards.

Signage was added throughout the campus to further wayfinding and identity, including a panel showcasing the school's history.

To create greater "curb appeal," the project team repainted the red, black, and white buildings in light and dark taupes with deep crimson red accents—a more sophisticated palette that helps to integrate the school into its environment and the surrounding community.

Each classroom in the new social studies building has clerestories and Solatubes—along with 8-foot-wide, 7-foot-high windows—that bring in abundant natural daylighting.

Each of the existing buildings on the campus had a window wall spanning the length of each classroom, providing daylight and outdoor views. This green modernization project replaced the clear window panes with two lower rows of translucent glazing and two upper rows of Solexia-tinted glazing to bring in abundant natural daylight while reducing interior solar heat gain.

Structural brace masked by greenscreen.

Green Modernization and Expansion School Projects

Typical classroom illuminated by solar tubes only.

Typical classroom with artifical lighting system on.

The artificial lighting system in all of the campus buildings was made more energy efficient and now has occupancy sensors that automatically turn off the lights in empty spaces.

Energy-efficient ductwork and HVAC equipment was installed in each of the campus buildings. Each classroom has individual HVAC temperature controls. The existing buildings have operable windows connected to the HVAC system. When the windows are opened, the air conditioning system turns off, saving energy.

The project team installed an energy management system on the HVAC and lighting systems that enables school administrators and the school district to measure and control energy consumption in each classroom.

The landscape architecture plan focused on mitigating heat islands throughout the campus by installing shade trees and large shrubs, including camphor trees, ash trees, magnolias, eucalyptus, *Carissa*, *Raphiolepis*, *Escallonia*, and *Dietes*. Turf was used in select multi-purpose gathering spaces.

The two main courtyards that serve the administration building and the gymnasium were given large shade trees, major turf areas, planters of flowers and shrubs, and seat walls to promote better pedestrian circulation and to support large student gatherings during lunch and before and after school. The smaller courtyards between each classroom building were landscaped with magnolia and ash trees, and seating to support their use as outdoor classrooms and informal gathering areas.

The new main pedestrian corridor through the campus was lined with magnolia trees in large break-out spaces to shade the pathway and provide gathering spaces for students between classes. The parking lots were landscaped with shade trees and islands of *Carissa* to also reduce the heat island effect.

The Westminster High School expansion is 26.6 percent more energy efficient than Title 24 requirements.

The expansion project also earned a CHPS rating under the pilot program for new buildings on an existing campus.

CHAPTER 12

Green School Trends

The state of green buildings—and public awareness about green buildings—has changed so dramatically in just the last few years that we've scarcely had time to catch our breath and recognize the new, more sustainable world that is evolving around us.

Expect changes in green schools to be just as dramatic in the near future. What can we look forward to?

Greater public awareness

Expect public awareness of environmental issues, particularly global climate change and the impact of buildings on human health, energy consumption, greenhouse gas emissions, and the environment to grow exponentially in the U.S. over the next decade, leading to much greater public demand for green buildings.

Paramount High School's gymnasium expansion, the Hall of Champions, was designed for CHPS Verification.

Greater public awareness will also generate a growing number of increasingly stringent green building, energy efficiency, and greenhouse gas emission regulations at the local, state, and national level, which will further the spread of sustainable buildings across the U.S.

A growing wave of green schools

College students are already asking college presidents and deans how green their campus is, and why it isn't as green as it should be. Parents of K–12 students are going to be asking their school districts the same questions, and demanding action.

According to the U.S. Green Building Council, nearly 1,000 school buildings in all 50 states in the U.S. have been registered for or have received LEED certification. More and more states have mandated that their new schools be built green, including Connecticut, Florida, Hawaii,

Top left, top right, and above: South Tahoe High School Career Technology Education Building was designed to CHPS standard.

Illinois, Maryland, New Jersey, Ohio, and Washington, as well as Washington, D.C. Many cities have committed to building green schools, including New Orleans.

Numerous school districts have already committed to using the LEED for Schools program in the construction and renovation of their schools, including Albuquerque, Anchorage, and Chicago. In California as of September 2008, 30 cities and counties had mandated some level of LEED certification for all public buildings, including schools.

Then there are the growing number of school districts adopting the CHPS program. CHPS has been adopted in eight states and by several community college districts. Currently, more than 30 California school districts require that their new construction and major renovation projects meet CHPS standards and earn CHPS certification, including Burbank, Long Beach, Los Angeles, Oakland, San Diego, San Francisco, and Visalia.

In July 2008, the Executive Council of the American Federation of Teachers adopted a "Green Schools and Colleges Resolution," urging state federations to advocate for their legislatures to adopt green schools legislation.

Compliance with the California Green Building Standards Code becomes mandatory in 2009. Meanwhile, the need to comply with California's AB 32 Global Warming Solutions Act of 2006 will soon generate new municipal, county, and state laws mandating green buildings.

The trend is clear: within the next three to five years, green schools will be the rule, not the exception. This is a huge wheel that has already started to move. Expect that movement to speed up exponentially.

Green modernization boom

The U.S. has more than 126,000 schools, which have a significant impact on energy and water consumption, greenhouse gas emissions, and human health and well-being. Expect green modernizations of existing schools to boom as school districts recognize the many benefits of having sustainable schools, and as more and more jurisdictions mandate green standards for major renovation projects.

The green modernization boom will also be driven by school districts that recognize that the most sustainable—and cost-effective—choice they can make is to carry out green modernizations of existing schools rather than to build new, or demolish existing schools and build new.

LPA used CHPS criteria in designing a joint-use library for the Paramount High School Senior Campus.

Left and right: Paramount High School Senior Campus library interiors.

Green School Trends

The main circulation corridor of the CHPS-designed Academic/Science building on the Paramount High School Senior Campus integrates daylighting strategies.

The best strategy is to create a district-wide green building modernization program. LPA, Inc., for example, created sustainability guidelines for the Long Beach Unified School District as part of its long-range facilities master plan.

Certainly, some schools have reached the end of their useful lives and should be demolished. The key is to demolish in a sustainable way and then construct a new green school on that site.

More joint-use schools

More and more cities and school districts will recognize the many benefits—from cost savings to open space preservation—of constructing joint use facilities at their schools, and they'll build accordingly.

More LEED schools

School districts have begun to recognize the value of commissioning and other aspects of the LEED for Schools application process, especially as state green school grant programs help to offset the costs of the application process.

A greater proportion of green schools will have LEED plaques in the future.

Function follows form follows function

As more and more green schools are constructed—and as more existing conventional schools undergo green modernizations—school districts will have a better understanding of what works and what does not work. The combination of performance and the synergy of green strategies will help guide future best practices.

In addition, the needs of increasingly demanding educational programs will shape the school of the 21st century, including student-centered learning environments, project-based learning, and "differentiated instruction."

These drivers, along with the emergence of innovative technologies, will generate a learning environment that looks and performs far differently from the 20th-century classroom, which will make these schools more sustainable and relevant to their times.

Paramount High School Senior Campus "Fieldhouse," designed for CHPS Verification.

Changing green school standards

Today's LEED-Platinum building will be tomorrow's LEED-Silver building.

Whether you're constructing a new green school or carrying out a green modernization of an existing facility, build flexibility into your school during the planning and design process so that it can easily and cost-effectively adapt to future changes in green building knowledge, design, technologies, standards, and regulations.

A financial shift in focus

More and more school districts will understand that, when it comes to new green construction, modernizations, and expansions, the *lifecycle* cost should determine the selection of materials, building systems, technologies, and school design, not just the upfront costs. They'll be looking at the long-term savings, as well as at the short-term costs, when creating a master plan for a green K–12 school.

New analytical tools

New tools are already under development and in use to give green school project teams and school districts a more in-depth understanding of the complex relationships between each component of a school campus and a green school master plan and budget, supporting key practices like lifecycle assessments.

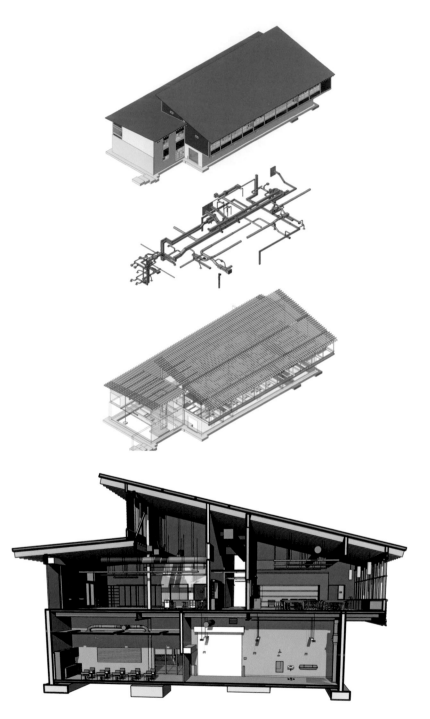

Top to bottom: The South Tahoe High School Career Technology Education Building.
The building's mechanical system.
The structure of the building.
BIM model of LPA's integrated design.

A BIM model showing integration of photovoltaic system on the roof of the Paramount High School Senior Campus Fieldhouse.

LPA, Inc., for example, uses Building Information Modeling (BIM)—a new model-based program that links with a project's database of project information. BIM generates a stronger quantitative and qualitative analysis of each aspect of the project and better design consistency. Thus, BIM enables LPA, Inc. and its clients to make better informed decisions about their sustainable building designs.

Mandatory "report cards" for school buildings

Dozens of cities and counties in California have mandated green building criteria for new construction and major renovation public projects.

As more and more government jurisdictions mandate green buildings, so, too, will more and more school districts adopt high-performance green building standards and set greenhouse gas emission reduction requirements.

California's AB 1103, the Green Building Initiative, requires that, starting in 2010, every existing commercial building must disclose its energy efficiency scores to prospective lenders, buyers, and tenants. Cities, counties, and the state will undoubtedly begin requiring energy efficiency scores for public buildings.

Expect in the near future mandatory "report cards" for school buildings that document their energy efficiency and greenhouse gas emissions, and mandatory report cards that document buildings' overall environmental performance.

The Academic/Science building on the Paramount High School Senior Campus.

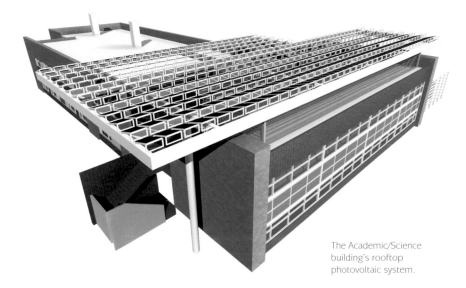

The Academic/Science building's rooftop photovoltaic system.

Net zero energy/grid zero schools

California's trend-setting AB 32, the 2006 Global Warming Solutions Act, which will be copied by other states in the coming years, focuses primarily on energy consumption, energy sources, and greenhouse gas emissions. With the connection between buildings and energy consumption and greenhouse gas emissions clearly established, expect California (and its followers) to enact legislation targeting these issues in public buildings, including schools.

The California Division of the State Architect, for example, has already created a "Grid Neutral Schools" plan and the business case for putting photovoltaic systems on school roofs to generate enough solar energy to meet their power needs, effectively taking them off the traditional energy grid.

The Los Angeles Unified School District is installing 1 megawatt of solar power at one of its schools, with a goal of installing 15 megawatts of photovoltaic systems district-wide.

The Academic/Science building's windows bring in abundant natural daylight into the interior, while sunshades help to keep out interior solar heat gain.

Increased water conservation measures

The Clean Water Act, maintenance requirements of mechanical water treatment systems, and long-term drought are combining to make school districts and green school project teams look at water consumption and treatment differently. Natural stormwater management and treatment systems—like bioswales, detention ponds, and manmade wetlands—will soon become the norm on school campuses.

Meanwhile, as drought conditions worsen in the western U.S., many school districts will make changes to their school athletic fields and landscape architecture to conserve water. Synthetic turf rather than grass playing fields, native and drought-tolerant grasses and plants rather than water-guzzling lawns and flowers, and water-conserving irrigation systems will become more widespread practices.

Joint-use gymnasium for Paramount High School designed for CHPS Verification.

Firm Profile

2008

American Institute of Architects
Committee on Architecture for Education
Merit Award: Santiago Canyon College Library

American Institute of Archiects
Orange County Chapter
Honor Award: Environmental Nature Center

American Institute of Architects
Inland California Chapter
Citation Award: Hawthorne Elementary School

American Institute of Architects
California Council/Coalition for
Adequate School Housing (C.A.S.H.)
Merit Award: East Natomas Education Complex
Merit Award: Marco Antonio Firebaugh High School
Merit Award: Melrose Elementary School

American Institute of Architects
California Council/Concrete Masonry
Association California/Nevada
Sustainable Merit Award: Marco Antonio Firebaugh
High School

2007

American Institute of Architects
Orange County Chapter
Honor Award: Palomar College LRC

American Institute of Architects
San Diego Chapter
Merit Award: Palomar College LRC

American Institute of Architects
California Council/Concrete Masonry
Association California/Nevada
Education Grand Award: Hector Godinez High School
Education Honor Award: Santiago Canyon College Library
Sustainability Merit Award: Santiago Canyon College Library

American Institute of Architects
Society for College and University Planning
(SCUP) Excellence in Architecture for a New
Building
Honor Award: Santiago Canyon College Library

American Institute of Architects
CORENET Global/IIDA Sustainable Leadership
Awards for Design
Award: Wal-Mart Experimental Supercenter

American Institute of Architects
California Council/Coalition for
Adequate School Housing (C.A.S.H.)
Merit Award: Laguna Beach High School Modernization

American Institute of Architects
American Association of School
Administrators/Council of Educational Facility
Planners International
Citation Award: Cesar Chavez Elementary School

American Society of Landscape Architects
California Chapter
Merit Award: Southwestern Community College Child Development Center

2006

American Institute of Architects
Orange County Chapter
Merit Award: Cypress College Maintenance & Operations Bldg.
Merit Award: Santiago Canyon College Library

American Institute of Architects
Inland California Chapter
Merit Award: Woodcrest Elementary School

American Institute of Architects
Central Valley Chapter
Honor Award: Wal-Mart Experimental Supercenter
Merit Award: LPA, Inc. Corporate Offices
Citation Award: Wal-Mart Experimental Supercenter

American Institute of Architects
California Council/"Savings by Design"
Citation Award: Sonoma State University Recreation Center
Citation Award: Toyota South Campus

American Institute of Architects
California Council/Coalition for
Adequate School Housing (C.A.S.H.)
Honor Award: Beverly Hills High School Science & Technology Center

American Institute of Architects
California Council/Concrete Masonry
Association California/Nevada
Education Grand Award: Sonoma State Recreation Center
Education Honor Award: Cesar Chavez Elementary School
Sustainable Grand Award: Sonoma State Recreation Center
Sustainable Honor Award: Cesar Chavez Elementary School

2005

American Society of Landscape Architects
National
Honor Award: Toyota South Campus

American Institute of Architects
California Council/"Savings by Design"
Merit Award: Cesar Chavez Elementary School

American Institute of Architects
Orange County Chapter
Merit Award: Cesar Chavez Elementary School
Merit Award: The Press Enterprise Headquarters
Merit Award: Orange Coast College "ABC" Science Building
Merit Award: Mt. San Jacinto College, Menifee Campus, Technology Center

American Institute of Architects
California Council/Concrete Masonry Association
Honor Award: Samueli Jewish Campus

American Institute of Architects
California Council/Coalition for Adequate School Housing (C.A.S.H.)
Award of Excellence: Thurston Middle School
Award of Honor: Woodcrest Elementary School
Award of Honor: Cesar Chavez Elementary School

2004

American Institute of Architects
Orange County Chapter
Honor Award: San Diego Jewish Academy
Honor Award: Tarbut V'Torah Upper School & Community Building at the Samueli Jewish Campus
Honorable Mention: Santiago Canyon College Science Building
Honorable Mention: Cuyamaca Community College Student Center
Honorable Mention: Shasta County Library

American Institute of Architects
Central Valley Chapter
Merit Award: Woodland Police Facility Headquarters
Merit Award: Grayson Community Center

American Institute of Architects
Redwood Empire
Citation: Sonoma State University Recreation Center

2003

American Institute of Architects
California Council/"Savings by Design"
Merit Award: Premier Automotive Group, North American Headquarters

American Institute of Architects
Orange County Chapter
Merit Award: Southwestern College LRC
Honorable Mention: Premier Automotive Group
Honorable Mention: Cypress College Maintenance Facility

American Institute of Architects
Long Beach/South Bay Chapter
Honor Award Green Architecture: Toyota South Campus

2002

American Institute of Architects
California Council
Merit Award: Mendez Intermediate School

American Institute of Architects
Orange County Chapter
Honorable Mention: Halford Residence
Honorable Mention: Hector Godinez High School
Honorable Mention: Fire Station No. 51
Honorable Mention: Pacific Coast Campus LRC

American Institute of Architects
California Council/Coalition for Adequate School Housing (C.A.S.H.)
Award of Excellence: Broadway/Golden Elementary School
Award of Excellence: Hector Godinez High School
Award of Excellence: Escondido Elementary Schools

2001

**American Institute of Architects
Orange County Chapter**
Honor Award: Mendez Intermediate School
Honorable Mention: Sage Hill School
Honorable Mention: Broadway/Golden
Elementary School

**American Institute of Architects
Long Beach/South Bay Chapter**
Honor Award: CSU Chancellor's Office
Honor Award: Broadway/Golden Elementary School
Merit Award: Temple Willow Maintenance Facility

2000

**American Institute of Architects
California Council/Concrete Masonry
Association**
Merit Award: Tarbut V'Torah Community Day School

**American Institute of Architects
Orange County Chapter**
Merit Award: TGS Irvine Corporate Campus
Merit Award: Escondido Elementary Schools
Merit Award: Temple Willow Maintenance Facility

**American Institute of Architects
California Council/Coalition for
Adequate School Housing (C.A.S.H.)**
Honor Award: Running Springs Elementary School

1999

**American Institute of Architects
Orange County Chapter**
Honor Award: Mission Imports
Honor Award: Mossimo Corporate Headquarters
Honorable Mention: CSU Chancellor's Office
Honorable Mention: Irvine Spectrum Fire Station
Honorable Mention: San Diego Jewish Academy

**American Institute of Architects
California Council/Coalition for
Adequate School Housing (C.A.S.H.)**
Award of Merit: Paramount Park K–8 School

1998

**American Institute of Architects
Orange County Chapter**
Honor Award: Tarbut V'Torah Community Day
School
Honorable Mention: Sage Hill School

1997

**American Institute of Architects
Orange County Chapter**
Merit Award: Mission Imports
Merit Award: Westwood Medical
Merit Award: Lake Hills Chapel

**American Society of Landscape Architects
Southern California Chapter**
Honor Award: South Chula Vista Library

**American Institute of Architects
Western Mountain Region**
Honor Award: Lake Hills Chapel

**American Institute of Architects
State of Colorado**
Honor Award: Lake Hills Chapel

**National American Institute of Architects
Religious Art & Architecture Awards**
National Award: Saddleback Valley Community
Church Interim Sanctuary

1996

**American Institute of Architects
Orange County Chapter**
Honor Award: Tarbut V'Torah Community Day
School
Merit Award: Saddleback Valley Community
Church Interim Sanctuary
Merit Award: Van Nuys Projects (Amtrak & DWP)
Merit Award: CSU Chancellor's Office
Honorable Mention: Anaheim Plaza
Honorable Mention: San Marcos City Hall

**American Institute of Architects
Orange County Urban Design Committee
Public Realm**
Merit Award: Tustin Marketplace
Merit Award: Anaheim Plaza

1995

**American Institute of Architects
Orange County Chapter**
Honor Award: Kubota Tractor
Merit Award: Spacesaver School
Honorable Mention: Lake Hills Chapel

**American Institute of Architects
San Diego Chapter**
Honor Award: South Chula Vista Library

Society of American Registered Architects
Award of Merit: CSU San Bernardino School of
Business

1994

**American Institute of Architects
Orange County Chapter**
Merit Award: Joint-Use Library, Rancho Santiago
College
Merit Award: Food 4 Less Retail Store

**American Institute of Architects
Central Valley Chapter**
Award: UC Davis Academic Surge Building

1993

**American Institute of Architects
Orange County Chapter**
Honor Award: Saddleback Valley Community
Church Interim Sanctuary
Honor Award: East Municipal Water District
Merit Award: El Camino Real Community Center

**American Institute of Architects
San Diego Chapter**
Citation of Recognition: Palomar College Wellness
Center

1992

American Institute of Architects
Orange County Chapter
Merit Award: Park Headquarters
Honorable Mention: Mission Viejo Town Center

American Institute of Architects
Central Valley Chapter
Merit Award: E. Coast National Scenic Area
Citation Award: Natomas Corporate Center

1991

American Institute of Architects
California Council
Honor Award: One Venture

American Institute of Architects
Orange County Chapter
Honor Award: Tustin Market Place
Merit Award: One Venture

1990

American Institute of Architects
California Council
Firm of the Year Award

American Institute of Architects
Orange County Chapter
Merit Award: Valley Telecommunications
Headquarters, DWP

American Institute of Architects
Cabrillo Chapter
Merit Award: Media City Center

1989

American Institute of Architects
California Council
Merit Award: River Center

American Institute of Architects
Orange County Chapter
Honor Award: University Montessori Preschool
Honor Award: CalMat Corporate Headquarters

1988

American Institute of Architects
Orange County Chapter
Honor Award: Galasso's Bakery
Honor Award: University Montessori Preschool

American Institute of Architects
Cabrillo Chapter
Merit Award: 100 Broadway Office

1987

American Institute of Architects
California Council
Honor Award: State Compensation Insurance Fund
Office
Merit Award: Renaissance Center Phase II

American Institute of Architects
Orange County Chapter
Honor Award: State Compensation Insurance Fund
Office
Merit Award: River Center Commercial Complex

1986

American Institute of Architects
Orange County Chapter
Honor Award: Calmat Corporate Headquarters

1985

American Institute of Architects
Orange County Chapter
Merit Award: Renaissance Center Phase II
Merit Award: Vintage Park Business Complex

1984

American Institute of Architects
California Council
Merit Award: Greystone Office Complex

American Institute of Architects
Orange County Chapter
Honorable Mention: Renaissance Center Phase II

1983

American Institute of Architects
Orange County Chapter
Merit Award: Subaru Distribution Center
Merit Award: Yuba City, City Hall
Honorable Mention: California Center

American Institute of Architects
The Masonry Institute
Honor Award: Yuba City, City Hall

1982

American Institute of Architects
Orange County Chapter
Merit Award: North Ranch Office Development

American Institute of Architects
South Bay Chapter
Commendation: Mission Park

1981

American Institute of Architects
Orange County Chapter
Honorable Mention: Greystone Office Complex
Honorable Mention: Larkspur Landing Retail

1979

American Institute of Architects
Orange County Chapter
Merit Award: Harold Hutton Sports Center

1977

American Institute of Architects
Orange County Chapter
Honorable Mention: Willows Retail

1971

American Institute of Architects
Orange County Chapter
Citation Award: LPA Office Renovation

SUSTAINABLE DESIGN AWARDS

2008

U.S. Green Building Council

LEED® NC Platinum: Environmental Nature Center
LEED® CI Certified: Surfrider Foundation

American Institute of Architects
Inland California Chapter/USGBC

Sustainable Architecture: Honorable Mention
CSUSB College of Education

Architectural Foundation Los Angeles

Design Green Awards: Citation Award
Environmental Nature Center

Concrete Masonry Association
California/Nevada
American Institute of Architects California
Council

Sustainable Category: Merit Award
Marco Antonio Firebaugh High School

Pacific Coast Builders Conference
Gold Nugget Awards

Best Sustainable Industrial/Commercial: Merit Award
Redding Library

2007

Concrete Masonry Association
California/Nevada
American Institute of Architects California
Council

Sustainable Category: Merit Award
Santiago Canyon College Library

CORENET Global/IIDA/AIA
Sustainable Design Leadership Award

Sustainable Leadership for Design Collaboration
Wal-Mart Experimental Supercenter

CHPS Collaborative for High Performance
Schools

Green Apple Award: Honorable Mention
Cesar Chavez Elementary School

2006

**American Institute of Architects
Central Valley Chapter**

Significant Work in Green Architecture: Merit Award
LPA, Inc. Irvine Office Headquarters

Significant Work in Green Architecture:
Citation Award
Wal-Mart Experimental Supercenter

**American Institute of Architects
California Council/"Savings by Design"**

Citation Award for Innovative Building Systems,
Natural Ventilation & Daylighting Strategies
Sonoma State University Recreation Center

Citation Award for Exceptional Performance
in a Large Suburban Office Park
Toyota South Campus

Sustainable Buildings Industry Council

Exemplary Sustainable Building: Second Place
Award
Toyota South Campus

Exemplary Sustainable Building: Honorable
Mention Award
Wal-Mart Experimental Supercenter

**Concrete Masonry Association
California/Nevada
American Institute of Architects California
Council**

Sustainable Category: Grand Award
Sonoma State University Recreation Center

Sustainable Category: Honor Award
Cesar Chavez Elementary School

**UC/CSU IOU Energy Efficiency Partnership
Program**

Best Overall Sustainable Design
Sonoma State University Recreation Center

2005

U.S. Green Building Council
LEED®– CI Certified: LPA Irvine Office Headquarters

**American Institute of Architects
California Council/"Savings by Design"**
Merit Award: Cesar Chavez Elementary School

2004

U.S. Green Building Council
LEED® Certified: Woodland Police Facility
LEED® Certified: Cotati Police Facility

**Pacific Coast Builders Conference
Gold Nugget Awards**
Best Sustainable/Green Non-Residential Project of
the Year: Toyota South Campus

2003

U.S. Green Building Council
LEED® Gold: Toyota South Campus

**Governor's Environmental & Economic
Leadership Award/California Environmental
Protection Agency**
Toyota South Campus

**Sustainable Design Leadership Award
CORENET Global**
Toyota South Campus

**American Institute of Architects
California Council/"Savings by Design"**
Merit Award: Premier Automotive Group, North
American Headquarters

**American Institute of Architects
Long Beach/South Bay Chapter**
Honor Award Green Architecture: Toyota South
Campus

2001

U.S. Green Building Council
LEED® Certified: Premier Automotive Group,
North American Headquarters

1992

**Southern California Edison
Design for Excellence**
Certificate of Merit: Irvine Ranch Water District

Sustainable Design Awards

SELECTED CHRONOLOGY

2008

Brea Sports Park
Brea, California

Irvine Valley College, Business & Technology Center
Irvine, California

California State University, San Bernardino,College of Education
San Bernardino, California

American Career College, Ontario Campus
Ontario, California

Surfrider Foundation Headquarters
San Clemente, California

20–40 Pacifica Towers
Irvine, California

Brea High School Brea–Olinda Unified School District
Brea, California

El Camino College, Humanities
Torrance, California

Cuyamaca College, Student Center
Cuyamaca, California

Mt. San Jacinto College, Technology Center
Menifee, California

Gauche Aquatic Park
Yuba City, California

2007

Heron Elementary School
Natomas Unified School District
Sacramento, California

Emulex Data Center & Offices
Roseville, California

Urban Decay
Newport Beach, California

Concordia University, Robert Alan Grimm Hall
Irvine, California

Blizzard Entertainment Headquarters
Irvine, California

College of San Mateo, Science Building & Planetarium
San Mateo, California

Press Enterprise Headquarters
Riverside, California

Hawthorne Elementary School
Riverside Unified School District
Riverside, California

Redding Library
Redding, California

Temecula Public Library
Temecula, California

BNC Mortgage
Irvine, California

Capital Group Company
Irvine, California

2006

Hesperia Civic Plaza
Hesperia, California

Lake Tahoe Community College, Learning Resource Center
South Lake Tahoe, California

Cypress College, Physical Plant
Cypress, California

CI Design U.S. Headquarters
Irvine, California

Santiago Canyon College, Library
Orange, California

Lakeview Elementary School
Placentia-Yorba Linda Unified School District
Yorba Linda, California

California State University, San Bernardino Student Union Expansion
San Bernardino, California

2005

Orange Public Library
Orange, California

Wal-Mart Experimental
McKinney, Texas and Aurora, Colorado

Mission Motor Sports
Irvine, California

Moreno Valley Sports and Community Center
Moreno Valley, California

Fiesta De Vida Master Planned Community
Indio, California

Eskaton Village Roseville, Master Planned Senior Community
Roseville, California

Santiago Canyon College Student Services Building
Orange, California

Las Positas College, Master Plan
Las Positas, California

Helen Keller Elementary School
Lynwood Unified School District
Lynwood, California

2004

Rancho Santa Margarita City Hall and Regional Community Center
Rancho Santa Margarita, California

Merage Jewish Community Center of Orange County
Irvine, California

LPA, Inc. "Sustainable Design Lab"
Irvine, California

Woodland Police Station
Woodland, California

Saddleback College, Health Sciences and District Office Building
Mission Viejo, California

Sonoma State University, Student Recreation Center
Rohnert Park, California

Legado Master Planned Community
Dayton Valley, Nevada

E*Trade Financial
Irvine, California

Cesar Chavez Elementary School
Long Beach, California

Desert Hot Springs High School Expansion
Palm Springs Unified School District
Desert Hot Springs, California

Laguna Beach High School Modernization
Laguna Beach Unified School District
Laguna Beach, California

Melrose Elementary School
Placentia–Yorba Linda Unified School District
Placentia, California

Witter Ranch Elementary School
Natomas Unified School District
Sacramento, California

Leona Jackson K–8 School
Paramount Park Unified School District
Paramount, California

Woodcrest Elementary School
Riverside Unified School District
Riverside, California

2003

Toyota South Campus
Torrance, California

Southwestern College, Learning Resource Center
Chula Vista, California

Almond Elementary School
Fontana Unified School District
Fontana, California

Norwood Middle School
Grant Joint Union High School District
Sacramento, California

Serra Catholic School Campus Master Plan
Rancho Santa Margarita, California

2002

Mission Viejo City Hall and Library Expansion
Mission Viejo, California

Santa College and Santiago Canyon College, Master Plans
Santa Ana, California

Skyworks Solutions
Irvine, California

Tarbut V'Torah Middle/High School
Irvine, California

2001

Premier Automotive Group, North American Headquarters
Irvine, California

Verizon Wireless
Irvine, California

Sierra Lakes Elementary School
Fontana Unified School District
Fontana, California

2000

Ross/Park Elementary School
Anaheim, California

Sage Hill School
Newport Coast, California

San Diego Jewish Academy
Del Mar, California

Selected Chronology

1999

California State University Chancellor's Office
Long Beach, California

Mission Imports
Laguna Niguel, California

Moreno Valley Public Safety Facility
Moreno Valley, California

Santiago Canyon College Learning Resource Center
Orange, California

Running Springs Elementary School
Anaheim, California

Ann Soldo Elementary School
Watsonville, California

1998

Anaheim Community Center
Anaheim, California

Paramount Park K–8 Elementary School
Paramount, California

San Juan Capistrano Community Center
San Juan Capistrano, California

Southern California College of Optometry
Fullerton, California

University Montessori
Irvine, California

Toyota Master Plan
Torrance, California

1997

Gemological Institute of America (GIA)
Carlsbad, California

The Chapel at Lake Hills Community Church
Laguna Hills, California

Mission Viejo Library
Mission Viejo, California

Mossimo Corporate Headquarters
Irvine, California

Tarbut V'Torah Community Day School
Irvine, California

University Research Park
Irvine, California

1996

Brea Community Center
Brea, California

Irvine Spectrum Pavilion
Irvine, California

Mission Viejo Town Center
Mission Viejo, California

Playmates Toys, Inc.
Costa Mesa, California

Rancho Bernardo Branch Library
San Diego, California

1995

Amtrak Commuter Station
Van Nuys, California

Anaheim Plaza
Anaheim, California

Chula Vista Library
Chula Vista, California

DWP Telecommunications Headquarters
Van Nuys, California

Faith Community Church
West Covina, California

Garden Grove City Hall
Garden Grove, California

Moreno Valley City Hall
Moreno Valley, California

Saddleback Valley Community Church Interim Sanctuary
Foothill Ranch, California

1994

San Marcos Town Center: City Hall
San Marcos, California

San Marcos Town Center: Community Center
San Marcos, California

San Marcos Town Center: Library
San Marcos, California

Temecula Community Recreation Center
Temecula, California

1993

ASK Computer Corporate Headquarters
Mountain View, California

Bumble Bee Corporate Headquarters
San Diego, California

Continental Retail
El Segundo, California

**California State University
School of Business and Information Sciences**
San Bernardino, California

Kubota Tractor Corporation
Torrance, California

San Bernardino County Law Library
San Bernardino, California

San Diego Gas and Electric
San Diego, California

Desert Vineyard Christian Fellowship
Lancaster, California

New Venture Christian Fellowship
Oceanside, California

1992

Burbank Gateway Center
Burbank, California

Irvine Ranch Water District
Irvine, California

North Island Federal Credit Union
Chula Vista, California

One Parkside
San Bernardino, California

Palomar College Wellness/Fitness Center
San Marcos, California

1991

Disneyland Hotel
Anaheim, California

El Camino Community Center
Orange, California

Natomas Corporate Center
Sacramento, California

One Venture
Irvine, California

1990

AST Research Corporate Headquarters
Irvine, California

Tustin Marketplace
Tustin, California

Vons Corporate Headquarters
Arcadia, California

1988

Calmat Corporate Headquarters
Los Angeles, California

E.R. Squibb & Sons
Irvine, California

River Center
Tuscon, Arizona

Tuscon Gateway
Tuscon, Arizona

DWP Sun Valley Distribution Headquarters
Sun Valley, Arizona

1987

Pod, Inc.
Santa Ana, California

1986

Tri-City Landing
San Bernardino, California

1985

Hutton Center
Santa Ana, California

State Compensation Insurance Fund
Sacramento, California

1984

Automatic Data Processing (ADP)
La Palma, California

California Center
Sacramento, California

1981

Greystone Phase 1
Las Vegas, Nevada

1979

Clubhouse V
Laguna Hills, California

1978

Chapman College Harold Hutton Sports
Center
Orange, California

Larkspur Landing
Larkspur, California

STUDIO

Principals

Robert Kupper
Dan Heinfeld
David Gilmore
James Kelly
James Wirick
Christopher Torrey
Steven Kendrick
Glenn Carels
Wendy Rogers
Jon Mills
Richard D'Amato
Joseph Yee
Charles Pruitt
James Kisel
Steven Flanagan
Karen Thomas
Don Pender
Kevin Sullivan
Kenny Lee

Associates

Brandon De Arakal
Chris Lentz
Young Min
Kenneth Murai
Patrick McClintock
Stephen Tiner
Carrick Boshart
Laura Nelson
Keith Hempel
Arash Izadi
Winston Bao
John Robison
Damon Dusterhoft
David Duff
Gloria Broming
James Raver
Lawrence Chiu
Michael Henning
Richard Bienvenu
Paul Breckenridge
David Eaves
Richard Musto
Stephen Newsom
Erik Ring

Staff

Lynette Stabile
Lorrie Ellis
David Olson
Kimberly Izadi
Robert Demmond
Deann Collins
Tracy Ettinger
Lisa Luttrell
Jeremy Hart
Wendy Robison
Casey Kysoth
Anna New
Tonya Pawli
Krista Smallwood
Nick Arambarri
Denise Mendelssohn
Jomay Liao
Kenneth Taylor
Justin Kerfoot
Silke Metzler
Michael Rich
Carlyle Aguilar
Mario Hernandez
David Diep
Craig Whitridge
Marc Pange
Kenneth Francis
Lili Ludwig
Nicole Mehta
Craig Shulman

Wendy Crenshaw
Adrienne Tabo
Robin Bugbee
Kimberly Coffeen
Lindsay Hayward
Karen Folsom
Michael McAllister
Ti Than
Dylan Blew
Carrie Carbajal
Mamerto Tabora
Wayne van Heel
Franco Brown
Noah Toomey
Asawari Marathe
Sylvia Situ
Kellie Moore
Paula Wallick
Patricia Rios
Rolan Castaneda
Myron Veazey
Ozzie Tapia
Heather Wills
Arturo Lavenant Jr.
Jason Willis
Yvette Sheehan
Jeremy Fong
Roger Van
Kimberly Hoffmaster
Daniel Chong

Samuel Sabin
Victor Giudici
Elizabeth Hatch
Stephen McMurchie
Stephen Thorlin
Andrea Blasko
Krislyn Flackus
Emiliano Melgazo
Charles Williams
Carrie Littlejohn
Samuel Lim
Jana Itzen
Rita Frink
Elaine Johnson
Douglas Cruse
Ana Lilia Mendoza
Renilio Cruz
McKenna Long
Brian Boyd
Heidi Roseler
Katherine Mraw
Renee Krause
Mina Roades
Andrea Peters
Fernando Calderon
John Gilmore
Stephanie Matsuda
Hye-Jin Sweem
Travis Rice
Marc Beique
Gretchen Zeagler
William Itzen
Kenneth Ong
Jin Seo
Angela Chiang
Chad Edgley
Jared Bohonus
Teresa McLean
Jessica Miller
Tamara Miller
Glenn Kubota
Marc LeGendre

Michelle Key
Trish Levoit
Andrea Larsen
Callie Gaillard
Nathan Pollet
Danielle Sedory
Luke Kinne
Ben Bravo
Hormoz Ziaebrahimi
Amy Harrington
Laurie Crutchfield
Melody Jiang
Jason Whitesel
Jim Gobright
Jill Kramer
Whitney Krudwig
James Maclay
Darcie Gumbayan
Lauren Moss
Morgan Amirani
Phan Chung
James Pinder
Alex Balais
Kristen Diedrichsen
Casey Chapin
Tracey Powl
Eric Jones
Naomi Robichaux
Jennifer Yarr
Tina Wang
Shawn Davidson
Ginger Shulman
Kristen Itahara
Tonya Miller
Emily Koch
Kyle O'Connor
Albert Lam
Megan Dietz
Andrew Wickham
Heather Zienowicz
Vernoica Namoc
Erica Lundblad

Heather Bohonus
Aaron Coppersmith
Jeff Mees
Tim Smallwood
Oscar Mendoza
Kami Bishop
Maria Louie
Elizabeth Cheng
Tyler Dick
Roy Matthew
Delores Mendez
John Wilson
Lindsey Engels
Anthony Harris
Phillip Lewallen
Kelly Angell
Miguel Cuevas
Gus Puertas
Cynthia Taylor
Andrew Cole
Monica Viramontes
Jessica Leonard
James Atienza
Dana Thomas
Douglas Seamark
Gary Williams
Rochelle Veturis
Tony Davis
Hilary Hynek
Mac Ruedas
Jose Rodriguez
Ryan Cadd
Judy Jacobs
Daniel Wang
Brian Parker
Louis Navarrete
Jonathan Linkus
Skye Paig
Lizeth Sandoval
Sarah Massey
Nick Ubrun
Fernando Cruz

Lancelot Hunter
Kimberly Thomas
Alan Gonzalez
Erik Lee
Dhruv Futnani
Donovan Helminiak
Grace Koo
Gary Friar
Kate Berezich
Kari Kikuta
Carlos Buenrostro
Chad Parson
Dan Pahlajani
Daniel Kang
John Rauh
James Ross
Shabnam Jahangiri
Maysoon Sheabaan
Matthew Arzt
Chris Coppersmith
Margarita Rivera-Smith
Esteban Rodarte

PHOTOGRAPHY AND DRAWING CREDITS

All drawings and renderings by LPA, Inc.
All photography by Costea Photography, except:

Page 11 top: Kellie Moore; middle: unknown; bottom: Adrian Velicescu

Page 21 bottom left and right: Kellie Moore

Page 33 bottom: Adrian Velicescu

Page 34 bottom: Adrian Velicescu

Page 35 top: Kellie Moore

Page 37 all photos: Kellie Moore

Page 38 middle: Kellie Moore